A friendly, readable style akin to a warm conversation telling the intriguing life of an extraordinarily simple, humble man. At the same time, it situates Brother André's life within the rich historical, cultural, and theological context that formed his compassionate and mystical spirituality. Blessed Brother André is experienced as a man of his particular time and place, the characteristic quality of beatification.

Rev. Hugh Cleary, C.S.C.
Superior General
Congregation of Holy Cross

A warm-hearted and inspiring picture of this Canadian Holy Cross brother who was regarded in his lifetime as a miracle worker, a loyal friend of Saint Joseph, and an agent of Christ's love and compassion to thousands of sick and suffering. Today, he is recognized by the Catholic Church as Blessed, the final step on the way to canonization, an honor for which this book clearly makes a persuasive case.

Rev. Edward A. Malloy, C.S.C.
President Emeritus
University of Notre Dame

Throughout her history the Catholic Church has always produced some altogether special men and women whose spiritual passion made them so different from their society that they appeared a little strange, walking their own marvelous way. Brother André was certainly one of them.

Gregory Baum
Professor Emeritus of Religious Studies
McGill University

Jean-Guy Dubuc's wonderfully accessible and insightful introduction to Brother André's life and his life's work provides its reader with a rich appreciation of this holy man's deep faith and extraordinary compassion.

Rev. Wilson D. Miscamble, C.S.C.
Professor of History
University of Notre Dame

Much more than a biography of a religious brother. . . . The reader walks away from this book not only knowing about Brother André's life, but more importantly about how simplicity conquered power, how hospitality overcame rudeness. This is a biography of faith manifested in goodness; it's a story we should all hear and try to emulate.

Rev. Richard Gribble, C.S.C.
Associate Professor of Religious Studies
Stonehill College

BROTHERANDRÉ

 Friend of the Suffering,
Apostle of Saint Joseph

Jean-Guy Dubuc

Foreword by Mario Lachapelle, C.S.C.

ave maria press AmP notre dame, indiana

First pubished by Éditions Fides, Montréal (Québec), under the title *Brother André* © Éditions Fides, 1999. Translation of *Le frère André* © Editions Fides, 1996.

Translation from the French by Robert Prud'homme.

This edition published by arrangement with Éditions Fides.

Foreword translated by Andre Leveille, C.S.C.

Foreword by Mario Lachapelle, C.S.C., © 2010 by Ave Maria Press, Inc.

Founded in 1865, Ave Maria Press is a ministry of the Indiana Province of Holy Cross.

www.avemariapress.com

ISBN-10 1-59471-190-9   ISBN-13 978-1-59471-190-9

Cover image © Joseph Métivier, C.S.C.

Cover and text design by John R. Carson.

Printed and bound in the United States of America.

PRAYER TO

BROTHER ANDRÉ

André, my brother . . .

You knew how to pray . . .
in the midst of your tasks, in the quiet of the night,
deep in your solitude, or surrounded by friends.
Teach me the words that nourish my soul.

You knew how to welcome . . .
the rich and the powerful,
the poor and the miserable,
the scholar, and the illiterate,
especially the simple, often the wounded.
Teach me to love them all without exception.

You knew how to suffer . . .
to hope in the future,
without complaint, without fear,
to stand firm, to face life.
Teach me the meaning of suffering in silence.

You knew how to live . . .
for the God whom you served,
for his Son and for his father and mother;
to save what is lost, to free what is shackled.
Teach me to hope in God and his universe.

CONTENTS

FOREWORD

MY FIRST CONTACT with Brother André's work goes back to 1966. I was eight years old and had a decent singing voice. My parents hoped I could become one of the Little Singers of Mount Royal and brought me to St. Joseph's Oratory to audition. I sang well but had a poor ear for music, a fact that became evident during the week of auditions. I left the Oratory after my short stay a little saddened, and yet the time there allowed me to get to know the miracle worker of Mount Royal and to see the pilgrimage place he had built in honor of his great friend, St. Joseph.

Instead of a career in the arts, I chose one in science and research. In 1989, while I was conducting research at the University of Montreal, I happened to glance out my office window one day and see the dome of St. Joseph's Oratory. It had been a long time since I had thought of it, and all of a sudden I wanted to see it again and to know more about Brother André's life and work. It was the beginning of something new in my life, which eventually led me to ordination and the vowed life in Brother André's religious family, the Congregation of Holy Cross. My Holy Cross superiors encouraged me to do graduate studies in theology, and I chose as a thesis to study Brother André's spirituality. I did this while ministering as a priest at the Oratory. In 2004, I was elected assistant general in Rome; the superior general of Holy Cross, the Very Rev. Hugh Cleary, C.S.C., assigned me to the overseeing of religious life and, more specifically, the causes for beatification and canonization. This is how—without my seeking it—I became the Vice-Postulator of Brother André's cause. In fact, I am the ninth person to hold that post since 1941.

A VICE WHAT?
AND WHAT WAS I TO DO?

The main responsibility of the Vice-Postulator is to assist the Postulator. This was given as my main responsibility from the very beginning. The Postulator of the cause, Dr. Andrea Ambrosi, stated more specifically what my work would entail: research, he said, all of the favors obtained since Brother André's beatification and see if any of the healings could be used for canonization. Brother André's beatification dated back to May 23, 1984, and a second miracle was needed by the Church for a possible canonization. My predecessor, Father Robert Choquette, C.S.C., Vice-Postulator from 1998 to 2004, had already prepared the way. There was one case in particular that he had focused on. A nine-year-old boy had been victim of an automobile accident, leaving him with a serious cranial injury and putting him in an irreversible coma leading toward death. The prayers of the people closest to him, along with the intercession of Brother André, brought him back to consciousness and health, and this was deemed scientifically unexplainable by many medical specialists.

This case occurred in 1999. This does not mean that before this date no other favors were obtained by Blessed Brother André. This particular case, however, met most clearly the strict criteria required by the Church. The time between the obtaining of a favor by an intercessor and its acceptance by the pope can be quite long and, for some people, too long. One must remember here that prudence is the mother of all virtues. For a healing to be declared miraculous and attributable to a servant of God, many systematic steps must be reached and certain conditions must be scrupulously adhered to. For example, the healing under study must be declared spontaneous, longlasting, scientifically unexplainable, and attained specifically through the intercession of the servant of God. It takes time to dismiss any reasonable doubt by a diocesan inquest before the case can even reach the Congregation for the Cause of Saints. In turn, the Congregation has to begin its own work in seeking a medical and a theological evaluation and, lastly, a third decision by a commission made up of bishops and cardinals.

WHY BE INTERESTED IN BROTHER ANDRÉ?

More than seventy years after his death, Brother André still has an important place in the memory and hearts of the people of Canada, New England, and beyond. His fame has far surpassed the frontiers of the places he lived. Evidence of this fame is seen in the faith of the people, expressed in thousands of letters along with millions of signatures petitioning for his canonization. All of this while keeping in mind that many witnesses who knew Brother André personally said that he never sought popularity or glory. He would rather have been in silent prayer than in the places of honor his superiors requested him to occupy. While participating in public celebrations, he was often seen among the people or behind his fellow religious—not among the dignitaries. The fresco behind his tomb signifies this by describing him as a poor, obedient, and humble servant of God. He probably often asked himself why such large crowds came and why they kept coming. Even now, each year more than two million pilgrims with different needs and ethnic backgrounds come to the Oratory in all types of weather, winter or summer, to ask for Brother André's intercession or simply to visit the shrine for the first time.

It must be said that Brother André in his life lived the gospel by showing his love of God and neighbor. He was a man of unconditional hospitality and compassion. Here let us look more closely at his words, as remembered by his friends and fellow religious.

AN INTRODUCTION TO BROTHER ANDRÉ'S SPIRITUAL MESSAGE

God is so close to us.

At a time when many Christians pictured God as a sovereign, Brother André told us that God was very near to us. He said that God was present in all of creation, and particularly in the human heart.

> "When you say to God, Our Father, He has his ear right next to your lips."

> "There is so little distance between heaven and earth that God always hears us. Nothing but a thin veil separates us from God."

God is good and he loves us.

For Brother André, God's love and forgiveness can never be spoken of too often. God is always working for our good, even when his actions seem incomprehensible to us. We must trust him because we are in his hands and he will never let us fall. God is free to do whatever he wills with all of his creation. He is not obligated to do anything for us. If God acts for our own good, it is by virtue of his immense goodness.

> "How good the Good God is! He really watches over us."

"People are worried for nothing. When help is needed, it will come in time at the right place by God."

No one is so small as to be excluded from God's love.

Everyone, without exception, is called to share in God's promises, love of life, and happiness given to all humanity. But God often uses the rejected, the little ones, and the forgotten to build his kingdom. They are his dear children because they are often most able to grasp his love and his message.

"It is with the smallest brushes that the artist paints the best paintings."

"Put yourself in God's hands; he abandons no one."

God invites us to become closer to him and to love him by loving each other as brothers and sisters.

For Brother André, all people are children of God and must consequently consider each other as brothers and sisters. Jesus, Mary, and Joseph incarnate the perfect model of filial love. We are invited to become members of this family by imitating it and by allowing our beings and our actions to be inspired by theirs, for this is how God's incarnation becomes close to us.

"God loves us so much! Infinitely! He wants us to love Him."

"Our Lord is our big brother. We are the little brothers, and we therefore have to love each other like the members of the same family."

"Practice charity with your neighbor—and this doesn't mean only to give money to the poor. There are many ways to practice charity. We could, for example, keep ourselves from examining our neighbor's conscience. There is also visiting the sick, who often do not need money, but who need good advice to help them get closer to God."

THE ORIGINALITY OF FATHER DUBUC'S WORK ON BROTHER ANDRÉ

And so, Brother André's work has strongly influenced the history of his people. It is said that more than one million people filed by his casket in January 1937. But we actually know very little about Brother André's interior life. We know so little because he left nothing written. Not even a line. Likewise, of the many biographies of Brother André—and in several languages—hardly any of their pages have been able tell us about his spiritual life. There is one important exception: this volume by Father Dubuc. In this, it differs from all the others. In my opinion, those who read it will come across something substantial when it comes to the miracle worker of Mount Royal.

I got to know Father Dubuc while he served as Director of Communications at St. Joseph's Oratory from 1994 to 1999. In his long career, which began in 1967, he has produced many meditations for television, film, and radio on the subject of Brother André and his work. This volume is without doubt one of his best works. As the Vice-Postulator of Brother André's cause for canonization, I strongly recommend this book.

Rev. Mario Lachapelle, C.S.C.
Rome
July 2009

INTRODUCTION

ONE CAN HARDLY give proof of the figures put forward for the estimation of crowds. They always remain approximate, often a very good estimate, but not scientifically foolproof. How, then, can one count the thousands of people who come to Saint Joseph's Oratory on Mount Royal, on beautiful summer days or chilly winter evenings, on foot, by car or bus? One can never measure their exact number, much less explain their very presence.

However, it is possible, without too great a risk of error, to say that some two million people visit the Oratory every year. This figure does not diminish, year in and year out; perhaps the contrary is true.

What can attract such crowds from all horizons to the Oratory?

Surely, something out of the ordinary. Or some extraordinary person.

This book wants to introduce that special person to you. At the outset, no one had any reason to place much hope in him. Yet, throughout the years, this wisp of a man embodied the hopes of millions of people. His name was Alfred Bessette; he became

1

known as Brother André. All those who came to him, and all those who still do today, found in him a reason or a way to live.

Millions of people know him today because they visit him at St. Joseph's Oratory in Montreal. They "visit" him? We could almost say that they "meet" him because he remains spiritually present to all who come and confide in him, telling their life stories, their troubles, and almost always their hopes. Not only in his large home on Mount Royal, which dominates the city, a main tourist attraction, but they also meet him in their hearts, memories, and prayers.

Blessed Brother André is part of all of these people's lives: they have real reasons to love him and to thank him. How many requests have been answered? How many cures have taken place here? No one can say, and we will never know for sure. Testimonies never cease to be heard in a variety of ways. It is through the generosity of these pilgrims with grateful hearts that this immense temple, the Oratory, was consecrated to St. Joseph, the father of Jesus. It is to him that Brother André gave his whole life and entrusted the cares of so many.

This small Holy Cross Brother was a most humble religious and yet very attentive to all who came to him. With very little education he became St. Joseph's "friend" and brought him the requests people confided in him. He merely wanted to build a simple devotional chapel, and yet he saw it grow into the largest shrine in the world dedicated to St. Joseph. It is also an exceptional spiritual meeting place for all seekers of faith. He never attributed any "power" to himself, and yet many wonders took place.

For a long time many of his followers have con-sidered him a saint. As it has often happened in the history of the Church, faithful followers precede Rome's decrees.

Blessed Brother André, so small, so timid, and so silent, still speaks to those who come to him, just as he did with those who came to him in the past. It is impossible to fathom the hearts of the pilgrims who found and who continue to find hope through their encounter with the man known as the "Mount Royal miracle-worker." But one may better understand them by reading, in the following pages, the strange story of his life.

CHAPTER 1

A GLORIOUS DEATH

"BROTHER ANDRÉ IS dead!" This was the headline, laid out in large black print, on the front page of the *Montreal Star*, *The Gazette*, *La Presse* and other Montreal dailies, on the morning of January 6, 1937. At the time, newspapers put out as many as three daily editions, allowing their readers to follow events as they unfolded throughout the day. As the death of Brother André occurred shortly after midnight, the morning papers first announced the news, and further editions supplied additional details all day long. In the very religious Quebec of the period, the event took on exceptional proportions.

Not just Montreal, but the whole province was affected by the news.

The Province of Quebec of that period was very faithful to its religious traditions. It was a time when the presence of the Church was felt everywhere in the everyday life of the French-Canadian people. At every level of social activities, the Church was present through its involvement in parishes, schools, hospitals, and various institutions. English Canadians referred to Quebec as the "the priest-ridden province."

The faithful flocked to parish churches four, five, or six times every Sunday, and often congregated during the week. Priests and members of religious communities were met with respectful greetings from all passers-by. The parish priest was often the most important man in town. To him, thorough respect was due. The Quebecois population trusted members of the Church unconditionally, as much for what they represented as a whole as for what they were individually: the élite of society. In short, the Church was at the time the unchallenged leader of the whole of Quebec.

Brother André, whose death made the headlines, was neither leader nor prelate. Yet, he was revered by all.

On the radio, broadcasters kept repeating the news of the day: "The Mount Royal miracle-worker passed away last night. . . ." No statesman or public figure could have drawn such attention. The person who had just died had touched the lives of hundreds of thousands of people, who, over the past fifty years, had visited him, sought his help, and prayed to him. He had listened to them. He had talked with them. He had shared their suffering and sorrow. Suddenly, these people felt alone, as if abandoned. Only Brother André could claim the affection of so many. He was the friend of thousands upon thousands of people, from the lowly to the mighty, from the downtrodden to the powerful, from the poor to the rich. He was unique, and now he was gone. He was leaving his friends behind.

During the preceding week, each passing day had brought more news of his agony, and every person who picked up a newspaper or turned on the radio was well aware of the imminence of his death. People knew that the ninety-one-year-old Brother was asking nothing for himself and was merely readying himself, as all mortals do, for his final hour. Yet many were numbed by a feeling of cruel shock and clung to the impossible hope that Brother André would grant himself the strength to go on, strength he had given to so many people in the past.

The Brother's body lay in state at the Oratory that he had founded. After his death, a million people tried to approach his mortal remains to express their gratitude. Had not Brother André, for the past fifty years, greeted and consoled crowds of visitors and sometimes even cured them? His fame had spread to the other Canadian provinces, to the United States, and even to Europe, making of him an internationally renowned religious figure.

Of course, some went to the Oratory out of sheer curiosity. Brother André had been the subject of so many stories, locally and internationally, that he had become something of a curiosity. His reputation as a miracle-worker, for some, and as a saint, for others, puzzled believers and unbelievers, scientists and ordinary folk alike. In almost every household, someone had a relative or a friend who had received a favor through Brother André in one way or another.

He also had his detractors, who thoroughly refused to acknowledge any of the spiritual realities linked to the founder of the Oratory. Such an attitude is comprehensible. The Church itself is very discreet and prudent when it comes to extraordinary signs that popular piety readily welcomes as miracles. Nevertheless, Brother André remained "the most popular Quebecois of all time," as the Sherbrooke daily *La Tribune* later put it.

On this cold week of January 1937, everyone wanted to see him. In the United States, where he was well known because of his trips and the friends he had made there, special trains were put at the disposal of visitors from the states of Maine, Massachusetts, Connecticut, Rhode Island, New Hampshire and Vermont. People also came by car, from all parts of Quebec and Ontario, on roads often made impracticable at that time of year. The Montreal tramways brought people in droves to the entrance of the Oratory, people who came, one last time, to pay their respects to a friend, an ally, a consoler, a savior, or simply an astonishing figure. A rich American came by airplane, for six days in a row, each time bringing with him people to honor the friend he had just lost. A man who was elbowing his way through the crowd toward the coffin said to the policeman who restrained him, "I'm a relative of Brother André!" which earned him the remark, "Today, everyone is a relative of Brother André. . . ."

It was freezing in Montreal, with sudden swings of temperature. The thermometer might go up a few degrees, but then an icy rain or sleet would pour down on mourners who spent hours getting drenched just to be able to see or touch Brother André's mortal remains for a brief moment. The crowds stretched from the street below to the very doors of the Oratory, way up on the mountain. To allow the greatest number of visitors to see him, a constant rhythm of 110 people a minute was maintained: thus, seventy-five to a hundred thousand people filed past him each day. On the day of the funeral, three times as many people tried to get close to the coffin. Never had such huge crowds gathered to pay their last respects to someone, be he a star, a hero, a politician, or a member of the nobility. Such mass mourning was never witnessed again in Quebec or in the rest of Canada. Those days form a distinctive part of our history.

Brother André was not embalmed, out of respect for his person. However, by order of the archbishop of Montreal, his heart was removed to be conserved for future veneration, according to a tradition still well alive in some European countries. His coffin was laid in the crypt in front of the main entrance to the Oratory. It was surrounded by hundreds of crutches, canes, and other objects left behind by grateful pilgrims.

Five hundred firemen and policemen were put to task to maintain order during the week that Brother André's body lay in state. Visitors, chilled to the bone, were requested not to stay more than a few seconds before the coffin of the aged Brother. Some wanted to touch him or leave a last request scribbled on a piece of paper. Others tried to carry off a souvenir, a "relic": their faith in Brother André's gift of healing was so unshakable that they felt a mere memento might be endowed with the same miraculous strength.

The witnesses of these moments kept with them the awesome memory of a national mourning shared by a multitude of intimate friends.

THE LAST DAYS

Brother André, surrounded by his close friend Joseph Pichette, a few of his brethren, three doctors, and two nuns, breathed his last breath fifty minutes after midnight on the day of the Epiphany.

He had been taken to the hospital five days earlier, when it became clear that the care he was receiving at the Oratory was no longer sufficient. His sickness was getting worse day by day. His remaining strength was rapidly failing him. The Brother's long pilgrimage was almost over; arrangements had to be made for his final rest.

On December 31, Dr. Lionel Lamy, his physician for the last several years, suggested to the Superiors of the Holy Cross Order that they transfer the ailing Brother to a hospital. It was feared Brother André would resist such a move. All his life, he had treated his body harshly, and he might still do so, to his last breath. But in his present state, he needed better care, which only the skilled personnel and the equipment of a hospital could ensure.

Doctor Lamy was the one who had to advise his patient of the transfer. He suddenly remembered something he had heard from a friend of the Brother. Joseph Pichette had told him that one day, while driving through the streets of Montreal with Brother André, they had passed by the small hospital run by the Sisters of Good Hope. The Brother had whispered, "What a beautiful place to die. . . ."

His doctor thus convinced Brother André to be treated in the very same hospital, which had seemed less forbidding than the others. By nightfall, he had already occupied one of the hospital's immaculate white rooms.

On the following days, his brethren and friends gathered to assist him, but there was no escaping the fact that the end was at hand. The Brother spoke little and suffered a lot. He told his Superior, "Sickness is a good thing because it helps us reconsider our past life and attempt some reparation, through suffering and repentance." Everyone considered him a living saint, but still he asked, "Will you please pray for my conversion?"

To the Sisters who cared for him and stayed at his side for long hours, he said, "It's a hard task for you to care for the sick." He told one of them, "Yours is a vocation of patience." The Sister answered, "Not so much as yours. Personally, I could not make myself greet so many people." And he replied, "Sometimes, it's very hard. If only people came straight to the point. But they insist on giving their names, saying where they come from, adding that they took the train. . . . Unfortunately, there's such misery!" To his very last moments, he remained himself: clearheaded with his visitors, somewhat impatient, but above all, compassionate.

Brother André, in the face of death, was like all mortals in their last moments: he was in pain, wary, conscious of his body, worried about his surroundings, much like all those people whom he had welcomed for some fifty years.

On January 3, three days before his death, he suddenly murmured, as if he had seen someone arriving, "The Almighty is coming. . . ." He knew the end was imminent. His long journey was almost over. He had been summarily baptized, the very day after his birth, because his parents thought he might die before his church baptism. Despite his fragile health, he had always eaten sparingly, often taking no more than some flour mixed with a little hot water. He had treated his body harshly, granting it little sleep or rest over the years. He had been said to be dangerously ill when he joined his community and yet had done countless jobs. And now, at the age of ninety-one, he was nearing the end of his long life.

On January 5, the hospital staff, well aware that only a few hours were left to the dying Brother, let some relatives, friends, pilgrims, and even a few patients from adjoining rooms visit Brother André. His brethren came to pay their last respects. Father Adolphe Clément, the first ally to Brother André's "mission" on Mount Royal, came to see him with the others. He had always been the most faithful of companions; he remained so, staying with his friend until the very end.

The hospital was besieged by visitors who had found some pretext to pay a last visit to the dying man. A Montreal radio station broadcast these comments: "In this city, in the entire province, people talk only of Brother André. Children stop playing to spread the news: 'You know, Brother André is dying. . . .' Old ladies go to church just to pray for him. Schoolchildren recite the rosary for him. In the streets, tramways and elevators, businessmen, shop girls, delivery boys, even unbelievers, everyone brings up Brother André's impending death. . . ."

Meanwhile, the subject of all these conversations suffered and worried about those who had to take care of him. "Sister, this is quite humiliating for you," he said to a nun giving him an injection. To the Sisters who shared with him their worries and hopes, he uttered the words he had repeated all his life, "Pray to Saint Joseph . . ."

On that day, the headline of the largest Montreal daily, *La Presse*, read, "Brother André at the Point of Death."

Dr. Lionel Lamy was by his side on the night between January 5 and 6. He later described the last moments: "And then, it was the end. In the last minutes of his life, there were three spasms, and his face contracted. The third spasm contorted his whole body and especially his chest . . ." At that moment, his old friend Joseph Pichette took to the Brother's lips the little crucifix he had been holding in his hands. Fifty minutes past midnight, on January 6, 1937, Brother André passed away.

Journalistic reaction to his demise might have seemed somewhat surprising had the old Brother not accustomed all those who knew him to things extraordinary or exceptional. For example, the Montreal daily the *Standard*, on the very day of his death, published a story right in the middle of its sports section, with this slightly puzzling title: "A Gentleman, a Sportsman, a Christian." And the story went on:

Today, people of all ethnic origins and religious creeds will be in tears, and a whole
city in mourning, as a beloved little old
man, Brother André, gentleman and saint,
will be buried. . . . And the author of these
lines knows that he cannot let this moment
pass without saluting this holy man, who,
during this writer's most somber and bit-
ter hour, reached out to him in friendship,
beyond the barriers of religious persuasion, with sympathy, warmth and encouragement.

Another newspaper, *L'Illustration nouvelle*, commented, "Workers have suffered an irreparable loss
in the passing away of this religious saint who was
always a friend for them. . . ."

Orner Héroux, one of the most brilliant journalists
of his time, published the following text in *Le Devoir*,
a newspaper traditionally catering to the city's intellectual élite:

This man's death triggers a deep and
sharp emotion. His eyes were but shut,
when droves of people found their way to
the Oratory, crowding around his mortal
remains. Amidst their grief, they offered
a quiet hymn of gratitude for all the kindness he had brought them. In all Catholic
circles throughout America, and perhaps
even abroad, the hearts of many will be
moved by the death of this man. . . . He
leaves behind him achievements that are
nothing less than exceptional: a monumen-
tal shrine which will defy the centuries
and an extraordinary spiritual heritage

that none can properly appreciate yet. In the heart of our province, on the mountainous flank of our great city, he has created a sacred place where hundreds of thousands of pilgrims converge each year. He has created a beacon of light, life, consolation, and hope that will shine throughout the continent. . . .

It is impossible to quote all that was printed. The personnel of the Oratory collected 860 newspaper articles from all over Canada and the United States, telling the story of the last moments of Brother André's life and that of his death. In France, the Paris daily *Le Figaro* stated, "An extraordinary miracle-worker has just died. Will Brother André be the first Canadian saint?"

Expecting great crowds of mourners, religious authorities thought it wise to hold two funeral services. On January 9, a first service was held in the cathedral, and a second, three days later, in the Oratory crypt.

The country's most prominent secular leaders, including the Prime Minister, the mayor of Montreal, several federal and provincial ministers, and some Members of Parliament, gathered at the cathedral to attend a funeral service presided over by the archbishop of Montreal.

After the ceremony at the cathedral, the funeral procession made its way to the Oratory, where Brother André lay in a mortuary chapel. Over the course of two days, three hundred thousand people came to pay him their last respects. It took the faithful close to six hours just to get from the street to the doors of the church, though the two were only about a third of a mile apart. The city tramways could barely handle the thousands of people who headed for the Oratory, despite miserable weather.

On Tuesday, January 12, the Archbishop of Quebec City, Cardinal Rodrigue Villeneuve, presided over the funeral service in the Oratory crypt. The Primate of the Canadian Catholic Church paid homage to the deceased and summarized the meaning of the Brother's life:

> On the tomb which houses the revered remains of the apostle of Saint Joseph, three words are inscribed: *Pauper, servus et humilis*. Poor, he was, the Brother whom you came to see on so many occasions. He was indeed a man of service, at the lowest echelon of his community. And he was assuredly humble, so much so that he never realized the breadth of his work or imagined that he could attract crowds. . . .

Later on, Cardinal Villeneuve told the Superior of the Oratory that, one evening, he had tried in vain to approach the coffin of the servant of God. The crowd was so dense that he was unable to clear a way for himself. The cardinal added, "I've often read, in the lives of the saints, of large gatherings of the faithful, which made it impossible for official personalities to approach the coffin of the revered dead. I always thought it was a pious exaggeration, but last night, I realized that it could be true."

Why such manifestations of popular mourning, such outpouring of affection for Brother André?

Perhaps because the little Brother gave special meaning to the lives of the people who loved him so much: he embodied their hope. He said only a few words to his visitors. He was never long-winded, and he always used speech and gestures sparingly. Yet, everyone seemed to leave him with rekindled strength and with a new reason to hope.

People were aware that he was just a poor little Brother with no education, diploma, or theology, but still they placed their utmost trust in him. His wrinkled face reflected years of work, suffering, illness, and that sadness common to all those who struggle. In reality, he was quite like the people who loved him so. And when he spoke to them, they believed him. He was one of them. They felt close to him.

And they knew they could go on hoping because of him. It was not uncommon to learn, either from a newspaper story or from conversations at home, of some extraordinary event witnessed at the Oratory. People spoke of miracles. And if one was unconvinced by such testimony, one could always go to the Oratory to catch a glimpse of all the prostheses hanging from the walls of the votive chapel. All of Brother André's visitors thought his gift of healing to be miraculous, long before the Church granted it any form of recognition.

They knew that the little Brother had been considered for several years to be a loser, scorned by society, helpless before authority. And yet, he had shown that despite all, one could hope, regardless of the severe judgments of men, regardless of human appearances.

In all of Quebec and beyond its borders, Brother André was reputed to be a miracle-worker. There emanated from this frail being, whose appearance was less than impressive, an exceptional spiritual aura that attracted crowds and left men of science dumbfounded, be they believers or not. Many recoveries, properly attested to by physicians, remained scientifically inexplicable. The only explanation was the power of faith.

There were also those who came to find solace, support, strength to go on living. For them, there were no spectacular recoveries, but newly found serenity. And it was a gift from the little Brother. Of the millions of people who came to the Oratory to see Brother André, very few actually recovered from physical illness. But all seemed blessed with renewed hope with which to carry on their lives. People went to him to be cured; they came away with the necessary strength to bear their affliction.

Brother André was always in the heart of those who had personal reasons to cherish him. For those who knew him less well, he remained an extraordinary human being. In the midst of those huge crowds of faithful admirers, often poor people ignored by science and society, there was perhaps an indistinct feeling of pride, or even of victory: Brother André was the living proof that the weak, the outcast, the poor could also achieve great and beautiful things.

Perhaps that is why two million people still come to visit him at Saint Joseph's Oratory every year. Out of curiosity, out of need, out of love, or simply to discover a reason for living, beside someone who knew that secret. To meet a kindhearted hero, whose love for others was a life-giving experience.

CHAPTER 2

YEARS OF POVERTY

ALFRED BESSETTE BEGAN looking for work in the early 1860s, going from one village to the next. Like so many of his countrymen, he was trying to escape the wretched poverty that had marked his childhood, poverty all too common at the time. Indeed, in those days, life for French-Canadian families was hard, in both urban and rural areas, and Alfred's family was no exception to the rule. The young boy had grown up, like so many children of his time, in conditions often discouraging, always demanding, and rarely gratifying. On the other hand, such a hard life created beings of a particular strength, characters as tough as the rocks in the plowman's field.

Alfred was born in 1845, in the village of Saint-Grégoire, in the Eastern Townships. He was the eighth child in his family. At the time, it was considered normal to have families of ten, fifteen, or even eighteen children. This way, farmers not only showed their faith in Providence but also made sure they had all the help needed for working the land. In fact, it was sorely tempting to take the male offspring out of school as soon as possible: they were the most accessible and the cheapest work force available. Why bother acquiring a higher education when one seemed fated to work on the family farm or destined to take up some trade linked to agriculture? Of course, in certain villages, the parish priest did occasionally take charge of a boy thought to be brilliant or studious enough to be worthy of a higher education, or even of the priesthood. But this was rather exceptional; ordinarily, the boys worked the land and the girls did household chores. In those times, one did not dare dream of the luxury of a higher education. Learning could hardly be construed as a means to self-fulfillment when people were struggling merely to survive.

YOUTH

Alfred's father, Isaac Bessette, was a construction worker. He also put his carpenter's skills to use by making household furniture. His trade forced him to move often, going where work was available. Alfred was only ten years old when his father died while cutting wood in the forest. His frail mother, Clothilde, who had given birth to two more children after Alfred, could not support such a large family on her own. She died two years after her husband.

At the age of twelve, Alfred was a poor, uneducated orphan who had no choice but to start working for a living. He no longer had a home of his own.

The day after his mother's funeral, the children were separated and taken in charge by other members of the family or by generous friends. They were offered a place to stay, with the understanding that they would help on the farm, in the workshop, or in their new home.

Years later, Alfred still recalled his mother's sweetness, which he thought she had lavished particularly on him. As he put it, "Probably due to the fact that I was the most sickly, my mother showed more affection to me than to the other children and also took greater care of me. She kissed me more often than I deserved. . . . And I, also, how I loved her!" Alfred even learned how to pray on his mother's knees. According to one of his friends, "Brother André always had a deep devotion to Saint Joseph, an inclination he owed to his mother."

His mother inspired in him more than religious devotion. She prepared him, through her own loving example, for a life devoted to the service of others, despite sickness and hardship. It seems almost surprising that the aged Brother should so insist upon his mother's tenderness, by remembering her countless embraces. A celebration, no doubt, of a kindness made all the more exceptional by the hardship his mother must have endured, raising several children and keeping house, while barely making ends meet. Of course, today, it is hard to grasp the colossal amount of work done by women in the households of old, deprived of all the comforts of modern life. The Bessette's house probably consisted of little more than a large living room, used alternatively as a workshop, dining room, and bedroom. As was

23

customary in those days, the mother managed the household, while the man of the house spent most of the day on the farm or in a workshop.

Instead of formal schooling, Alfred learned from his mother's example: her strength and love readied him for a life devoted to the care of his fellowmen. Perhaps he was more touched by his mother's qualities than were his siblings because of his own frailty, or because of some particular expectation of his. In any event, his mother's memory never left him, and she remained forever close to his heart. At the end of his life, he explained, "I've rarely prayed for my mother, but I've often prayed to her."

When his mother died, little Alfred lost both his love and his home. Fortunately, one of his mother's sisters, Marie-Rosalie, wife of Timothée Nadeau, took the child in her care. The orphan found a new family with the five Nadeau children. A new life started for him, in a new world.

At the time, the Province of Quebec was known as Lower Canada. In 1840, it was unified with Upper Canada, mostly made up of the present-day Province of Ontario. With this union came representative government, in which Quebec had its share of Members of Parliament. Its inhabitants aspired to live in a climate of peace with their English-speaking neighbors, despite the fact that the latter were also their conquerors. After the 1837 Rebellion, during which French-Canadian "Patriots" had risen against British rule, the British Parliament strove to find a common ground between "the two nations" of the country. The population of the Eastern Townships was composed of old French settlers and of newly arrived English landowners who had been generously endowed by their government. Close to the American border, whole villages were populated by Loyalists who had fled the new American republic.

Canada still had a struggling economy. The countryside was especially poor. To survive, courage, determination, and hope for better times were needed.

Like the rest of the Western World, Canada was beginning its Industrial Revolution. The installation of machinery in factories was about to transform traditional industries. The transition was difficult, both in towns, where new industries were implanted, and in the country, where people struggled to adapt to a new economic context.

Like most boys his age, young Alfred quickly left school to work on the farm. To be independent in a turbulent world, he had to find a way to make a living. And these were troubled times indeed. The traditional society of Quebec, ever faithful to Church teachings, which stressed conservative values and wariness of liberalism, was undergoing quite an upheaval. It was a time of turmoil and shock, as a whole society strove to adapt to radically changing times without ever relinquishing its old values.

The mid-nineteenth century brought wretched poverty to Canada's rural areas. In the region south of Montreal, where the Bessette offspring were loosely scattered, life was hard, as it was everywhere in the countryside. Work was difficult to come by and given only to the strongest, the most gifted, and the most ambitious. People left their farms to seek employment in town. Montreal, populated by 60,000 mostly English-speaking inhabitants in 1851, saw its population

swell to 260,000 by 1901. In the mid-1800s, when
Canada was still known as British North America,
its entire population totaled one million and a half,
of which 650,000 lived in Lower Canada—later to be
called the Province of Quebec.

Alfred did not feel at home in this world of
aggressive competition. Trying to survive, he went
from one job to another. He tried his hand at a dozen
different trades, wandering from town to town. With
no education or trade, he could only do menial tasks
and obtain unsteady jobs. Bakers, cobblers, tinsmiths,
and blacksmiths hired him, but always and only as
an apprentice.

In such a context, Alfred's future prospects were
very limited. He could rely only on his courage and
tenacity to earn his daily pittance, in increasingly difficult conditions. His driving strength was his will
to live, despite all hardships. Already at this stage in
his life, he harbored a deep faith in God, whom he
recognized as his Master. His faith was inseparable
from an intense love of life, which gave him the
strength to conquer all obstacles despite his limited
means. He was also driven by the deep conviction
that he could do something to change things. Due to
his delicate health, he could not master some of the
trades he might have adopted. Much later, in one of
his rare comments on his youth, he explained why:
"Repairing shoes on your knees, holding a hammer
all day long, that hardly favors your digestion."

In these circumstances, it is scarcely surprising
that Alfred ventured to the United States to find
work, like thousands of others.

Why such a sudden move to find employment across the border?

There were two reasons. The first was the situation in Canada, where only the wisest and the best trained were able to earn a living within an evolving economy. These were not ordinarily the kind of people found deep in the countryside. A sickly young man, with no family, no formal education or trade, was bound to be even less fortunate than others were. So he might as well look abroad, where new opportunities abounded.

Equally important was the fact that the United States had entered the Industrial Age far more rapidly than had Canada. Its new industries, facing a labor shortage, promised ideal, indeed extravagant working conditions to all new laborers. It is hardly surprising, then, that many young Canadians left their farms and families behind in search of opportunity. Of course, when one had neither land nor family, expatriation seemed all the more tempting.

At twenty, Alfred Bessette set out for the New Hampshire factories. He was like many young men his age, who decided to take matters into their own hands, rather than be left out in their own country. Several thousand of them emigrated, either alone or with their whole family. One trait was common to them all: they had a good deal of courage. At the turn of the century, there were as many French Canadians in New England as in the whole of Quebec! Alfred could thus hope to meet up with some of his relatives and Canadian acquaintances. In fact, several members of his family followed his example and moved definitively to the United States. These emigrants came to their new country with scant possessions; yet, they held on to their traditional family and cultural values, one of which—perhaps the strongest, the most important—was their religious faith. For a long time, though, there were no Catholic churches in those parts, churches where the newcomers might come to pray or simply to feel at home. This must have come as a big disappointment to Alfred, steeped as he was, from his youngest years, in religious devotion and prayer.

From very early on in his life, Alfred had shown a definite religious inclination. The Phaneuf family, with whom he had worked and lived, left us this description of him: "He was a very sickly young man. He could digest practically nothing. He rarely went out. But he was very kind, and he was always praying." Friends of the time also remembered that he was given a nickname, "Saint Joseph's fool." Such a cruel expression was meant to ridicule a devotion or piety rarely seen in boys his age. On the other hand, this little witticism also reveals Alfred's determination to voice his feelings clearly and to take his place among his peers. As can be seen, even in a strongly Catholic society, religious fervor could raise eyebrows.

In New England, particularly in the states of Connecticut and New Hampshire, the cotton industry was booming. In Moosup, Hartford, and Phoenix, where workers were being hired by the hundreds to man newly built factories, Alfred offered his services and his youthful enthusiasm.

Little is known about the few years the young Canadian worker lived in exile. He talked very little about them, and no witness to this part of his life was ever found. But the working conditions of the time are well documented. Apprentices worked twelve-hour days, six days a week, with a half-hour lunch break, all for a dollar a day! For Alfred's rest, a small rented room surely would have sufficed. It would have been quite modest, considering his meager wages. But he would have been the last person to complain. Had not the Nadeau family, who had adopted him after his mother's death, sometimes found him sleeping on the floor, in a spirit of mortification? It had been his way of praying. Thus, in America, it seems unlikely that he should have resented modest living accommodations, having never wished for, let alone known, much comfort in his childhood.

The work and life of mill workers were altogether uneventful. Men worked to survive, with no time or strength left for leisure. On Sundays, the only day off, those who lived close to a church attended Mass and vespers. And they tried to gather enough energy to get back to the grind the next day.

French Canadians living in New England had various meeting places where they shared their joys and sorrows. All exiled people, who have left behind lands and relatives they may never see again, know how important mutual support is. At first, the newcomers met in their own homes; later, they congregated in parish halls. Gradually, French-Canadian culture spread to parts of New England. Villages grew where everyone spoke French. These attracted French-Canadian priests; while Mass was still said in Latin, the sermons, at least, were delivered in French. Eventually, village life took on an almost

French-Canadian flavor in New England. Many decided to call it home, and these people became known as the "Franco-Americans."

In the years when Alfred was working south of the border, many of his peers still suffered from the separation from their families and pined for their homeland. In 1867, Alfred may have heard, from one of his fellow workers, of a new era of hope dawning in Canada, with the recent proclamation of the Confederation. There was talk of going back to the native soil; soon people began moving back home. After seven years of loneliness, and perhaps of longing, Alfred decided to end his sojourn in America and to return to Canada.

Exactly where should he go? Alfred decided to go where he still had emotional ties. His first stop was Sutton, right across the American border, where part of his family lived. A little while later, he was in Farnham. But finally, he settled in Saint-Césaire. And, in that village, Providence revealed itself by way of Father André Provençal, an old acquaintance of Alfred, whom he had often visited in his presbytery before leaving for the United States.

FATHER ANDRÉ PROVENÇAL

In 1867, with its 4,000 souls, the parish of Saint-Césaire was quite important. The village itself was traversed by the road leading to the growing city of Sherbrooke. Some English-speaking families lived there, but it was predominantly a French-Canadian village. Young Alfred, freshly returned from exile, could not have helped but notice its beautiful new church.

Also prominent in Saint-Césaire was Father Provençal himself, whose energetic personality rubbed off onto his parishioners. The church was barely finished when the parish priest launched another project, the building of a convent for young girls. On the day of its inauguration, in 1857, the convent had already attracted 150 boarders. Twelve years later, Father Provençal opened a "commercial college" for boys. These were impressive achievements in a small village quite far from Montreal. Father Provençal must have been a convincing man when it came time to approve church projects. Alfred Bessette was drawn to this generous man; he hoped the priest might guide him as he faced the uncertainties of his new life, which seemed to him no less bewildering than his American adventure had been.

Land was plentiful in the region, but Alfred did not have the heart to be a farmer. The immense expanse of the fields was certainly more of an inspiration for meditation and prayer than had been the tarnished walls of factories. Although Alfred knew enough about farming to make a living from it, he preferred to spend his time near the presbytery doing odd jobs. After all, he was not asking for much in life. He had learned how to live sparingly and knew how to make what little money he needed to survive.

The Canadian economy and population were growing quite rapidly, despite considerable emigration to the United States. Still, rural areas remained impoverished, and a farmer's life was anything but easy. There was more time for leisure than there had been at the cotton mills. However, the workday was as long on the farm as in the factories, and real respite came only in the off-seasons. Money was scarce, so expensive distractions were out of the question. People spent their spare time at home, among friends, or engaging in parochial activities. Life revolved around the parish church, which helps explain the great influence the local priest had on his flock. This, of course, also favored Father Provençal; with his bent for leadership and his reputation as a holy man, he might well inspire all those around him. Alfred, in particular, did not escape his influence.

He was often seen at church, praying or helping in small chores. The church might well be the village's hub; it was still unusual to see a man of Alfred's age go to the presbytery on a regular basis or pray so often in church, be it at the main altar or in front of Saint Joseph's statue. Alfred must have known that he might be singled out and taunted for his behavior. In his later years, however, the Brother never mentioned having suffered because of his peers. Somehow, he must have been quite like his friends, and yet, at the same time, very different from them.

In those days, young people courted each other at their respective homes, under the watchful eye of their parents. It was normal for them to prepare for their marriages and families, as had their parents and countless generations before them. Not so for Alfred! His love went out to the people he had learned about on his mother's lap, people who had become his steadfast childhood companions. Their names were Jesus, Mary, and Joseph, the members of the Holy Family.

Obviously, such unusual behavior in a young man attracted the attention of the parish priest. One day, Father Provençal learned that Alfred often stayed late at night in the barn, praying on his knees in front of a cross put up with the farming tools. He prayed to the point of exhaustion, people said, judging from his deathly pale face and his pitifully weak body. The priest also found out that Alfred was hiding under his shirt one of those iron chains used for harnessing horses: he wore it against his skin, just as certain mystics of old wore hair shirts. The priest admonished him severely: "You've got no right to do such a thing!" Only a man like Father Provençal, who was as close to God as to his fellowmen, could temper with such authority the excessive impulses of a generous heart.

Father Provençal quickly realized that this generosity could be channeled in a more positive way. Had Alfred ever hinted to him that he felt drawn to the religious life? Perhaps. He certainly did not have the necessary education or preparation to become a priest. Perhaps a Brother, then? But even those who knew him well and measured the extent of his piety thought Alfred to be too ignorant to become a man of the cloth. All those they knew, after all, had studied for years before becoming teachers in schools or colleges.

And yet, as one of Alfred's nieces put it much later, "He always said he felt at his happiest among priests, at church, and during devotional offices." One of his best friends testified during the procedures leading to his beatification, "I believe Brother André was convinced he was not made to live in the secular world." So perhaps Alfred did aspire to a religious life, even as he measured the obstacles on his path. His firm resolution to achieve his goal against all odds may have been a convincing argument in his favor. Father Provençal, who was aware of Alfred's profound aspiration, told one of his friends, "I'll see to it he finds a proper place. . . ."

And where might that be? In Montreal, right across from Mount Royal, at Notre-Dame College, a school run by the Congregation of Holy Cross. The good priest had written to the college authorities, "I'm sending you a saint. . . ."

CHAPTER 3

THE BROTHER
PORTER

WHEN ALFRED BESSETTE arrived at Notre-
Dame College, on November 22, 1870, he was
twenty-five years old. He had nothing to his name,
and he harbored in his heart the rather extravagant
hope of being accepted as a member of an institution specialized in the education of young boys. It
must have taken unshakable faith in his protectors,
Saint Joseph and Father André Provençal, to even
dare knock at the college door. What could a reticent
country boy, who had trouble reading, bring to such
an institution? The only books with which he was
familiar were the Gospels, which he knew practically by heart. He was learned only as far as the life
of Jesus was concerned. Father Provençal must have
written a glowing letter of recommendation to the
college Superiors for them to admit Alfred. Indeed, at

the outset, he simply was not qualified to enter any religious community.

However, some weeks later, on December 27, Alfred Bessette entered the novitiate, a probationary period for young members of religious orders. With his admission as a novice came two distinctive signs, which he was never to relinquish. He wore a black cassock, tied at the waist with a black cord. He also took a new name, signifying he was leaving one world to enter another he had freely chosen. He chose the name André.

Why exactly André? In honor of Father André Provençal, the very man who had led him to the threshold of a new life. Until then, Father Provençal had always been at his side, the better to guide him. Now, everything was in his own hands. He had to fashion his own life, using what resources he possessed. And, by most people's standards, those resources seemed limited indeed.

The young Brother was well aware of his limitations. However, deep down, he must have been convinced that his life could be changed for the better. He had not joined a religious community to find a haven, but rather to do something useful. He would not have become a man of the cloth had he not thought he could help others. How? He did not know. He had to invent his own future. By joining a religious order, he had shown his faith in Providence, which had guided him so far. He had also shown great faith in his own ability to serve Providence through his care for those entrusted to him.

THE PORTER

Several years later, as an elderly Brother, he recalled, "When I first came to the college, I was shown to the door . . . and I remained there for forty years!" It is a fact: all the time he spent working at the college, he was the porter, the gatekeeper, that is. He would open the college gates, welcome and direct people to their destinations. These tasks could be mastered without a diploma: the only requirements were flexibility, patience, common sense, and humility. And he was endowed with all these qualities. For many years, he was simply known as Brother André, the porter.

Of course, a porter does not merely stand guard over a door, day in and day out. His Superiors gave him other duties to keep him busy: he was a nurse, a cloakroom attendant, and a light man, and he was entrusted with keeping the community hallways tidy. He was also called upon to sweep the chapel, the college corridors, rooms, staircases, and so on. It all made for a rather special kind of novitiate! In fact, his workload was excessive; no wonder his brethren found him unusually frail and fragile. Brother André later explained to one of them, "I never refused any of the work I was asked to do. I always said Yes, and I would finish at night what I could not complete during the day."

In fact, by fulfilling his various tasks, Brother André was scrupulously following the rules set forth by his community, which prescribed detailed descriptions of tasks for its members. It is instructive to consult these regulations, as they were formulated within the Constitution of the Holy Cross Order:

854— There shall be in each house important enough to require it, one or more Brothers entrusted with opening and closing the entrance door, receiving strangers, attending to letters, packages, errands, and, generally, to anything addressed to the house; these Brothers will also ascertain whom is being asked for, and will introduce strangers, only inasmuch as this would be necessary.

855— For this, it is indispensable to have trustworthy Brothers, of a modest and composed exterior, who are active and intelligent, polite and honest, accustomed to receiving people respectfully, knowing how to tactfully refuse requests without disgruntling the unfortunate visitor; discreet, speaking only of what is appropriate, and to the people concerned only, incapable of taking the liberty of reading any newspapers, letters or notes with which they may be entrusted.

856— They shall be housed near the doors to which they have to attend, and shall never leave these doors open longer than is necessary; they shall take their meals in their lodge, and there also shall they pray, examine their conscience, and embark on spiritual reading. . . .

857— They shall never accept anything without verifying the name of the sender. . . .

858— They shall always keep the reception rooms and parlors clean, well ventilated and lit, and shall open and close them accordingly. . . .

865— Should poor people come to the door, porters shall receive them with kindness, remembering that Jesus Christ is hidden under the rags of poverty. . . .

These prescriptions are precise and very detailed concerning courtesy, protocol, and good order. Brother André, as a good postulant, strove to fulfill all his duties exactly as his Superiors expected.

However, a year later, just as he hoped to be officially admitted to his congregation, its provincial council rejected his candidacy in these terms: "Brother André is not permitted to take his temporary vows because his health does not allow us to think he will ever be admitted to the [Perpetual] Profession."

The novice must have been bitterly disappointed. In fact, Alfred was convinced he had already become Brother André. As far as he was concerned, his future life was to be at the service of the Church and totally detached from worldly things.

He was heartbroken, but certainly not defeated. He had gone through frustrating experiences in the past, be it on the farms of Saint-Césaire or in New Hampshire factories. Through it all, he had learned how to overcome all obstacles in his way.

A few weeks later, the Bishop of Montreal, Mgr. Ignace Bourget, came to Notre-Dame College on an official visit. Heedless of protocol, Brother André contrived to approach the prelate and talked to him about his hopes and his present state of confusion. "I knelt before him, with my clasped hands on his knee. Mgr. Bourget spoke to me like a father." The bishop was swayed, and he assured the little porter that "the community would keep him. . . ."

It took a lot of courage and audacity, considering the times, to dare go over the heads of his Superiors and directly appeal to the bishop. More than audacity, actually: his actions showed his determination to reach his goal within the Church, that of being of service to others. Even if this meant challenging his peers, going against established opinion or traditions. Certainly, he knew his limits, yet he could never be deterred when he was convinced his cause was just. Everything he undertook, over the course of his life, was fuelled by this single-minded determination. Unable to persuade through speech, he would often resort to clever yet inoffensive ploys to reach his goal—all the while remaining faithful to his vows of obedience. At the outset, he may well have appeared to be a loser. However, time would show the extent of his final victory.

The Master of Novices, who was well aware that Brother André was being counted out in the novitiate, said to his Superiors, "If this young man is one day unable to work, he will at least know very well how to pray." And it was for this sole reason that he was allowed to take his temporary vows. Then, on February 2, 1874, at the age of twenty-eight, Brother André took his perpetual vows, committing himself forever to a religious life.

Again, he had reached his goal against all odds. He no longer worried about his ultimate commitment or about the meaning to be given to his life. His deep faith and unflagging assurance may explain the special kind of humor with which he entertained his fellows. His occasional flashes of wit delighted the whole community.

At the time, Notre-Dame College was home to 150 boys, all of them boarders. In addition to the tasks already given him, Brother André, by now a true jack of all trades, was assigned to the barbershop. (As shall be seen further on, this assignment proved one day to be very useful.) Brother André had become a very busy man! Where did he find time to pray? At night, in moments stolen from his sleep on the bench in the porter's lodge. This meant little rest and a lot of work for a man in poor health.

The young Brother's diet only compounded his health problems. He ate sparingly, usually taking nothing more than a piece of bread dipped in some watered-down milk or soup. Frugality was an integral part of his life, the more so because of the symbolic significance he gave to it. Christ had suffered for sinners, and his own life must be similar to that of his Master.

This very simple form of spirituality was an essential component of his religious commitment. He wanted to be united with Christ through suffering. Why? To be like Him. To be with Him. This way, he could pray all day long, everywhere, always. His friend Azarias Claude recalled, "I don't think Brother André ever neglected his duties so that he could go to the chapel to pray. He often said to me that it was possible to pray anywhere, even while working, so that one did not even have to go to a chapel or church to pray." After having gotten through his daily chores, Brother André would venture to the chapel, and there, most often by night, converse with his God.

Thus Brother André led an uneventful life; his brethren were sometimes hardly aware of his presence. All this was to change, of course, as he began surprising those around him.

ASTONISHING RECOVERIES

While at the infirmary watching over a few patients, he came to the bed of a boy who, under doctor's orders, had been lying there for the last several days because of a strong fever, and said to him, "Why are you being so lazy?" To which the child replied, "But I'm sick." "No, you're not. . . . Why don't you go and play with the others?" And the boy, feeling a sudden strength, got up and joined his friends, to the astonishment of students and professors alike. The Brother's gesture was not appreciated. He was accused of being imprudent and of interfering with the work of the head nurse. The boy was thoroughly examined, but not a trace of his former illness could be found. A doctor even checked in on him several times a day, expecting some sort of relapse. But there was none. The sick boy was cured, and no one really knew how.

This incident is one of the first cases of healing reported in the life of Brother André. The boy was among the very first persons to be cured thanks to his personal intervention, in a way that none could explain and fewer still tolerate. In the opinion of his brethren, the little porter could hardly claim to possess the power of faith healing, much less of influencing the normal course of nature. As other cases occurred, a certain animosity flared up in the congregation.

Some of Brother André's remedies were something of an embarrassment to his fellows. On some occasions, rather than simply declaring a patient cured, he used—or suggested using—an oil that had burned under Saint Joseph's statue. He called it simply "Saint Joseph's oil" and recommended rubbing sick limbs or wounds with it. This prescription rapidly earned him the nicknames of "Old Smearer" or "Old Greaser"! Of course, the events taking place under the very eyes of his brethren were very hard to explain. It was therefore normal to regard them with amused, if not mocking, skepticism.

On the other hand, many must have been aware of the special curative powers already attributed to "Saint Joseph's oil," both in Canada and in France, by those people who had prayed for Saint Joseph's intercession. Certain cases were well known, even within the college community. For a long time, Brother André had developed a special devotion to Saint Joseph. Could he not entrust him, then, with the care of the suffering? And if Saint Joseph so pleased, he could very well answer his prayers! Notwithstanding, many remained unconvinced. Why would the Lord elect Brother André to relieve human misery? A person of rank, a scientist, or some well-known virtuous soul would have seemed a more obvious choice.

The Brother porter surely must have been upset by the attitude and comments of his brethren. Yet, he certainly gave no sign of it. Moreover, it never stopped him from listening to the suffering, or being attentive to their misfortunes and encouraging them to pray to Saint Joseph.

One of his biographers related the following incident, said to have taken place in 1884. He heard it from a companion of Brother André and vouched for its authenticity. Brother André was busy scrubbing the floor at the entrance of the college when two men came in, carrying a woman crippled with rheumatism. She begged to see Brother André so that he might cure her. He said to the two men, "Let her walk by herself." She managed one step, then another and another; all the while the Brother kept on scrubbing the floor. After a while, he said to the woman, "You're no longer sick. You can go home now." And she left, completely cured.

Another extraordinary event, which occurred at about the same time, bears a strange resemblance to an episode from the Gospels. It is worthwhile quoting the whole story, couched in the picturesque prose of Azarias Claude, who heard the tale from the very person concerned:

> A man from out of town had two boys at Notre-Dame College. He went to visit them every week or fortnight and would meet Brother André each time. The Brother invariably greeted him so: "How is it going?" To which the man would answer, "It's going fine." On one occasion, the Brother added, "And how is it going at home?" The answer was terse: "What business is it of yours?" The man went in to

see his boys. On his way back, Brother André said to him, "You seem to be in a bad mood." The man shot back, "Who wouldn't be?" The Brother went on, "Well, what's the problem?" And the answer was, "I have two boys at school here, and it's costing me plenty. My wife has been sick for years . . . and needs a nurse to care for her. Then, there are the doctors, who cost a bundle. . . ."

The man kept on walking toward his carriage. . . . Brother André followed him out. The man seemed to be in a hurry. Brother André told him, "At this very moment, things are getting better at home. Next time you come to see your boys, tell me how everything went. Goodbye!"

. . . At about the same time Brother André was talking to the husband, the man's wife, who had been bedridden for years, asked her nurse, "Bring me a chair, will you? I want to sit in my room." To which the nurse replied, "But you can't even get up!" The woman answered, "Yes, I can. I feel better." And she was brought her chair. The sick woman told her nurse how suddenly well she felt. She went on to say that she wished to go out onto the porch for some fresh air. And she got up and started walking. She went to sit on the front porch and waited for her husband to bring her news of her boys.

All the while, our man was heading home, with not a clue as to what had happened there on that very day. As he got closer to his home—a secluded house away from the road, with a large front porch—he could see that there was someone on the porch, but could not imagine it might be his wife. But as he got closer, he did think he recognized her.

When he finally arrived, he leapt from his carriage and ran to the porch. And it was indeed his wife! How he must have regretted the sharp words that he had spoken to Brother André. . . .

People spread stories such as this one far and near, and the reputation of Brother André grew, whether he liked it or not. More and more people asked to see him or talk to him. They sought his help for their own sake or for the sake of their loved ones. By 1890, his influence was undeniable: the college lodge was besieged daily by crowds of insistent visitors.

At first, the school authorities did not particularly object to the situation. They knew Brother André would never betray their trust. But soon the schoolboys' parents objected. They disliked seeing their children so close to sick people, who, they feared, could easily transmit their diseases to them. The parents threatened to withdraw their children from the school, since they were being offered no protection from the Brother porter's unfortunate visitors.

Even in his own circle, Brother André had developed something of a bad reputation. For instance, no sooner had Dr. Charette, the college physician—and steadfast foe of the porter—coined the nickname of "Brother Greaser" than people were repeating it wherever the porter went. Visitors coming out of the porter's lodge overheard comments like, "There goes another one who just got greased!" It was even said, "At first, whoever went to see Brother André ran the risk of being portrayed as a madman." Brother André was also criticized for receiving ladies in the room he used as an office, although on such occasions he was never without a witness. He adhered to this chaste rule all his life. For all of this, what could he say? What could he do?

As one of his brethren put it, "Brother André used to weep. Simply because he was so hurt. But he never criticized anyone, and he never held a grudge."

His burden must have been hard to carry. It must have taken great inner strength, deep faith, and exceptional courage to persevere on this mission, which everybody—with the exception of the sick—seemed intent on impeding. His habitual humility put him at a disadvantage as he tried to defend his care of the sick against his brethren's opposition. How could this ignorant and insignificant porter claim to refute the arguments of his wiser peers?

It took more than simple courage to go on. It took the firm belief that he was doing God's will. Brother André must have felt, deep in his heart, that he was serving God, albeit in a very particular way, and that he had to fight to do so. Like Jesus in the Garden of Gethsemane, he wept, he trembled, he suffered, but in the end, he chose to embrace his destiny. As shall be seen further on, Brother André, in his imitation of Christ, most strongly identified with its outcome: the Passion.

Partly to appease his critics and partly to protect the Brother porter, the college Superior reached an original solution. In 1893, a new tramway line was inaugurated, linking downtown Montreal to the small neighborhood of Côte-des-Neiges. After negotiations between the college and the tramway companies, it was decided that the "cars," as they were then called, would go by the school. A shelter was built right in front of the college for eventual passengers, although they were, in truth, few and far between. The Superior suggested that Brother André use this new tramway stand to greet his visitors. Thus the sick would no longer disturb the students, their parents' concerns would be allayed, and a safe distance would be put between the porter and some of his unduly critical brethren.

The tramway stand became Brother André's first reception room, as it were, and he used it as such for a dozen years, until he managed to have a new one built on the mountain, next to the Oratory.

This was something of an obsession for Brother André: he wanted to build a chapel on the mountain facing the college, where the faithful would come to pray to Saint Joseph.

Easier said than done. First, his community had to own the land; this came about in 1896, when the Holy Cross Congregation acquired a big section of the lands facing the college, behind the tramway stand. Then again, one had to have the means to construct this chapel, humble and small as it might be. Finally, Brother André needed backing: from his Superiors, obviously, but also from some good people who would use their influence and money to further the construction. The dream seemed far off. But it was always on Brother André's mind. And he knew that Saint Joseph, to whom he wished to pay tribute, was very close to him. Were not all the marvelous deeds due to the saint's intercession sufficient proof that he could ask of him anything? In his distinctive fashion, Brother André set to work: in silence, prayer, and faith in his own mission.

In the evenings, the Brother porter would set out, sometimes alone, sometimes with a few pupils, and he would climb the mountain. Slowly, pathways were formed. And each time he climbed, Brother André would strew on the ground medals of Saint Joseph, as if to give him the land, or at the very least, to consecrate it to him.

Each day, through the window of the college lodge, he could see the side of the mountain that he wanted to offer to his patron saint. He went one step further, acting with the same naive faith which had inspired him since his childhood: he placed a statue of Saint Joseph looking toward the mountain. Thus the saint could see, far ahead of time, the place where Brother André wished to lead him and prepare himself for the journey.

CHAPTER 4

THE IMPORTANCE
OF FRIENDS

IN THE SPRING of 1922, a biography of Brother André was published in Toronto, bearing the title *The Miracle Man of Montreal*. Its author was George H. Ham. In the introductory pages, he wrote: "Whether the reader believes or not in present-day miracles or in the invisible power of the 'Miracle Man' is a matter of little consequence. But I must admit that, while I do not practice the same religion as my old friend, I have witnessed some of the miracles chronicled in this book. . . ." As this passage shows, it was not for reasons of faith or religion that Col. Ham rallied to Brother André's defense. It was out of friendship.

Three years later, a New Yorker, William Gregory, wrote his own book about the Brother. The author wished to rectify certain erroneous information allegedly given to American visitors at the Oratory. Gregory claimed that as many as three hundred thousand Americans visited the Oratory in 1924 alone. He wrote: "If this narrative leads American tourists, especially those not of the Catholic faith, to better understand the great work being carried out in this citadel of belief, I shall feel that my effort has not been in vain." In his book, Gregory also came to Brother André's defense simply out of friendship, moved by an affection that transcended the barriers of creed or denomination. In fact, friends of the Brother often voiced their support for his work, and this from its very inception. Without their assistance, his dream never might have materialized, and the Oratory never might have been built.

TOGETHER

At the dawn of the twentieth century, Montreal was a city swept by rapid change. During the preceding decades, the Industrial Revolution had depleted the countryside and drawn countless farmers to urban areas. In 1901, Montreal was the most important city in Canada, with a population of 267,730. The ethnic origins of its citizens were varied, but for the first time in more than a century, the "French" outnumbered the "English." Even as their numbers were proportionally dwindling, the English held the upper hand in the economy of the province. Most often, they were the progeny of well-to-do immigrants, such as businessmen or industrialists. The English attended only the best schools; they mastered the intricacies of the financial markets, held the highest positions in the key sectors of the economy, and discreetly controlled commerce. Several factors had contributed to this economic disparity. The greater part of the French population of Montreal had arrived freshly from the countryside. Since the English Conquest in 1760, French Canadians had been more or less abandoned by their new government. They never had received any kind of help, be it in the form of funding or social services. Thus, most French Canadians did not go beyond grade school, with some noteworthy exceptions: the most brilliant or wealthy students might aspire to a liberal profession or to a career in the Catholic Church.

The poorest of these people worked in factories, which brought them little hope of future prosperity. Working hours were long, and social welfare policies were virtually nonexistent. Moreover, they still had to support large families, as they had done for countless generations on the farm.

The small French-Canadian bourgeoisie, industrious as it was, was kept at arm's length from the decision-making circles of big business. Apart from a small élite of liberal professionals, most French Canadians held humble positions. Those who did not make up the bulk of the unskilled workforce were local merchants or low-ranking civil servants and public service employees. They worked hard for little money, and their jobs were rarely rewarding.

Brother André knew many such people. They might be parents of the college students, neighbors in what was then just the village of Côte-des-Neiges, or simply men and women who visited and trusted him. All of them were his friends.

And he always embarked on his most ambitious ventures with their support.

Ambitious as they may be, Brother André's enterprises always began with one small step. He had already taken that first step when, in his porter's lodge, he had set a statue of Saint Joseph facing the mountain. But that was just the beginning. He then decided to nestle the statue in the hollow of a tree, beside one of the paths he had cleared in the woods now owned by his religious community. Brother André often went to that spot to pray, either alone or with pupils or visitors. But he wanted more than just a nook for Saint Joseph. He wanted a chapel dedicated to him. To put Saint Joseph on his side, he scattered medals of the saint on his path as he wandered on the mountain, medals that would one day pave the saint's way. He even called the biggest, most important path leading to the statue "Saint Joseph Boulevard."

When Brother André first proposed building a hillside chapel, his Superiors flatly rejected the idea. He did not argue his point further. That was simply not his way. He searched for other avenues to reach his goal. Here is an example of one of the mild ploys he used instead of verbal persuasion, an anecdote we owe to Brother André himself.

Brother André, while still the college porter, could often be found praying on the mountainside. Noticing his absence from the college refectory, one of his brethren came to fetch him in the woods, and found him kneeling on the ground. "Brother André, why aren't you at the college? It's suppertime!"

"But I can't leave. Saint Joseph wants me to promise him to build his chapel. . . ." The repartee must have been repeated throughout the community.

In 1902, Brother André suddenly fell ill and was bedridden. Next to him in the infirmary was none other than the college Superior. The two men quickly struck up a friendly conversation. Brother André pleaded his cause with such enthusiasm that he managed to persuade his Superior, and he got the permission to build a chapel dedicated to Saint Joseph on the mountain.

To be more precise, permission was granted, but no more than that, not even a penny. Brother André also received the following advice: "Tell Saint Joseph construction can begin as soon as you find the money!" It seems that Brother André had foreseen this turn of events. Indeed, he had long ago obtained from his Superiors permission to keep the small amount of money he earned while working as a barber, charging five cents per haircut. After many years of work, he had managed to put aside no less than $200: a fair amount, but not nearly enough to build an Oratory.

Brother André began scavenging for construction materials and asking for volunteer labor. His closest associate in his enterprise was Brother Abundius, the college carpenter. The man was a master when it came to general construction or woodwork. He had filled the classrooms with handmade chairs and desks and had repaired anything that needed fixing in the college. Not content with practicing Saint Joseph's trade, he even sported a beard much like the ones traditionally found in the saint's iconography. He was also, like Brother André, a detached, simple, and generous person. The Brother could not have found a better man to put in charge of the initial construction.

Work began. First, the volunteers chopped down trees, in order to widen the path that already cut through the forest, leading toward the future chapel. They had to make do with simple, if not rudimentary, tools, and the slope of the land only made their job a little harder. Then, they cleared a larger perimeter of land intended for the building of the chapel itself. Eventually, more trees would have to be felled to provide the necessary space for those people who would attend chapel services, for Brother André was absolutely convinced that pilgrims would come in droves to pray to Saint Joseph in these woods.

Brother Abundius worked hard, but it seems that Brother André himself seldom did any actual construction work. He was, of course, unfamiliar with the trade itself. And he had to fulfill all the other tasks assigned to him at the college. As well, he was kept all too busy attending visitors—which he did for hours on end—and visiting the sick. So, for his project, he would offer prayers and words of encouragement and the hope that bolsters any resolve.

One day, Brother André was called to the bedside of a certain Calixte Richard, an expert mason. The man was grievously ill: he had a tumor in the stomach. The Brother greeted the mason with words rapidly becoming habitual: "You're not sick!" And he told the man's wife, "Give him a good bowl of soup."

The patient protested, "But I can't swallow a thing!" Brother André took the emaciated man by the hand, led him to the dinner table, and asked him,

"Should Saint Joseph heal you, would you come and help me build a chapel on the mountain?"

"Of course I would," replied the incredulous mason.

"Well," the Brother continued, "I'll see you in the morning, then. . . ." And the next day, as Joseph Pichette remembered it, "This man Richard came to eat breakfast with Brother André at six-fifteen in the morning. He worked all of that day and for several more months without ever feeling any pain." Calixte Richard recruited some of his friends to assist in the construction work. And he became a good friend of Brother André.

The land where the new building would stand was cleared in a few weeks. It was time, finally, to start building the chapel itself. The work was over within eight days. Of course, the chapel was quite small: it stood twenty-five feet high, twelve feet wide, and sixteen feet long.

Brother Abundius later recalled, "The construction of the little chapel was financed by private donations. It took seven or eight days to build, on our free time. Brother André was convinced the chapel would eventually have to be enlarged, but he was still happy with the modest beginnings." The chapel could hold no more than ten people. Its facade was entirely made up of two wide doors, which were swung open for open-air Masses.

The building was extremely simple. The outer and inner walls were coated with corrugated iron. Since there were no windows, sunlight trickled into the chapel from the rooftop, through bits of frosted glass. There was not even a steeple, just a simple cross.

Still, the new building drew some reviews. On October 7, 1904, Montreal's most popular newspaper, *La Presse,* carried the following story:

> On Wednesday—the very day dedicated to Saint Joseph—the staff and students of Notre-Dame College will inaugurate, by means of a procession and solemn Mass, a chapel built on the mountain facing their monastery.
>
> From the tramway line, one can see the modest building, nestled like a little hermitage in a cluster of birches and pine trees. The cross on top of the roof is fifteen feet high, and can be spotted easily over the treetops. By building this chapel, the Holy Cross Congregation wanted to show its gratitude for the countless favors due to Saint Joseph's intercession, and thus pay a special homage to its patron saint.
>
> This chapel, dedicated to Saint Joseph, will be unique in its kind in Canada. Pilgrims will travel here from all parts of the country to venerate the saint, and to plead for his intercession. . . . The plans were drawn up by Rev. Brother Abundius and the work supervised by Rev. Brother André.

Another paper, *La Patrie,* described the consecration the very day after the event:

> On the mountainside adjacent to the village of Côte-des-Neiges, there now stands a magnificent chapel dedicated to Saint Joseph.

Several hundred of the faithful gathered this morning in the chapel of Notre-Dame College, as Mgr. Racicot, vicar-general, blessed a statue of Saint Joseph.

After the ceremony, a large procession made its way up to the hillside chapel.

Four Brothers of the Holy Cross Congregation triumphantly carried the newly blessed statue. In front of them, the cross. Behind them, the college students, some members of the clergy, and the faithful. . . .

The vicar-general congratulated the Holy Cross Congregation for taking the initiative of building a new chapel dedicated to Saint Joseph, and for finding such a beautiful setting for it. . . . Before ending the ceremony, the preacher praised the virtues of Saint Joseph and invited the faithful to address their prayers to the great saint.

These articles are remarkable in two ways.

First, great importance is given to the inauguration of what is, after all, only a small, humble chapel. One must remember how very religious the French-Canadian people were at the beginning of the century. At the time, all church activities aroused considerable curiosity and interest. A new building on the slopes of Mount Royal—even in what was then only a village, and not yet a Montreal neighborhood, Côte des Neiges—would quite naturally draw considerable attention, especially when one considers how devoted Catholics were to Saint Joseph, the patron saint of Canada.

Another detail strikes the attentive reader of these articles. Little case is made of Brother André's personal role in the erection of the chapel. No mention is made, either, of the crowds that, for the last several years, had been coming to see the Brother at the college or at the tramway stand. Why such a silence?

Above all, it bears witness to Brother André's humility. He always behaved with the utmost discretion as his dream slowly took shape. He would have been the first to rejoice in seeing his community receive great credit for his own efforts: never once did he promote the idea that the Oratory was in any way his personal achievement. It even comes as something of a surprise to see him described, in one article, as a supervisor of the construction work. He did everything in his power to ensure that the chapel would come to be, but he never had anything to do with its actual construction.

Since Brother André never talked about his role in the project, his brethren could hardly be expected to acknowledge his efforts. At the time, Brother André was still no more than a modest porter, credited only with attracting gullible people desperate to share their woes with someone. He had yet to receive any kind of public acclaim, let alone to be hailed as a miracle-worker. Thus, it is quite normal that the newspapers of the day should hardly mention him. For no one could imagine that a man as unassuming as Brother André could be the spiritual founder of a chapel "unique in its kind in Canada," as one of the journalists had put it—with as much naiveté as unwitting prophecy.

From its very inception, the Oratory was a communal project. Brother André's friends, be they laymen or clerics, gathered around him in order to give form to his dream. Of course, the man behind the project was, and remained, Brother André. But he only wanted to build a house of worship as humble as Saint Joseph himself. He never dreamt that his simple chapel might one day become a magnificent church. There is proof of this. When the construction work ended, there were a hundred dollars left from the donations collected, and Brother André, convinced he would no longer need the money, simply handed it to his Superiors.

Very soon, it became obvious that the little chapel was far too small for the crowds it attracted. No less evident was the fact that pilgrims would arrive during the wintertime as well as during the summertime. It might be asking a lot of the faithful to have them attend open-air Masses during Montreal's icy winters. Three eminent Montreal citizens thereupon submitted a joint request to Father Georges Dion, the Provincial of the Holy Cross Congregation. They were Césaire Lemay, a contractor; Jules-Aimé Maucotel, a deputy city registrar; and T. A. Durand, a merchant. All three were good friends of Brother André, and they fully endorsed the project of building a larger chapel. In fact, what they had in mind was an edifice that would further encourage the devotion to Saint Joseph: a real church dedicated to him. And to this end, they asked for not a penny from the congregation.

Father Dion, acting on his sole authority, could not possibly endorse this project. He suggested that the three emissaries take their petition to the archbishop of Montreal. The latter approved the project, with the stipulation that it should come under the authority of Notre-Dame College. However, the congregation simply could not afford the financial guarantees that this arrangement implied. Undaunted, the three petitioners rallied the support of other impassioned businessmen. They successfully argued their case in front of the college authorities, without at any time involving Brother André in these discussions. As a result, in August 1908, a new, larger chapel was inaugurated. It could hold about a hundred people. On the day after its inauguration, however, seven hundred people tried to get in! From then on, large crowds gathered there every Sunday. The chapel seemed as small as ever.

The problem had to be addressed immediately. This time, sixteen zealous laymen came to the rescue of the faltering project, promising to "further the work on Saint Joseph's Oratory." They presented a written request to Father Dion, begging his permission to "build housing for two people, near the Oratory, so that the former may safeguard it and ensure that the house of worship remain open throughout the winter months." Two thousand people eventually signed the petition. And permission was granted to build yet another chapel.

To this end, parts of the existing chapel were salvaged. After removing its large front doors, it was used to form the choir of the new building, to which a nave was added. Altogether, the construction cost $5,000. The new chapel was inaugurated on November 22, 1908. A sacristy and a steeple were added in 1910. In the shadow of the great basilica, this building still stands today, a timeless legacy of Brother André's friends.

The same committee also decided to build a small visitors' pavilion beside the chapel, in view of offering various services to pilgrims. Of course, the college authorities still oversaw the work in progress. In 1909, there was an operating deficit of $1,400, and the archbishopric resolved to hand over definitively the Oratory bookkeeping to the college bursar.

That same year, Brother André was relieved of his duties as a porter and became the "keeper of the Oratory." The help, loyalty, and determination of his friends finally had earned him a mission which, actually, he felt unworthy of, that of being totally at the service of the pilgrims of the mountain.

FRIENDS FROM ALL
WALKS OF LIFE

All his life, Brother André relied on many precious friends. Some were irreplaceable because of the resourcefulness or fervor that they brought to his cause. Joseph Pichette was one such man.

In 1911, Joseph Pichette was only twenty-five years old and already a condemned man, according to his doctors. Despite his physician's entreaties, he decided, as a last resort, to solicit Brother André's help. He visited the Brother at the Oratory and declared that only death could force him to take his leave of him. Brother André took him at his word. Cured by the end of the week, Pichette remained, up until the Brother's death, the most loyal of friends.

He was the Brother's chauffeur when the former went to see people too sick to travel to the Oratory. He was also his confidant, as they drove for long hours through the streets of Montreal. He came to know most everything about Brother André's life and later would recall in detail how the Brother had spoken to the sick, how he had urged contrition and prayer.

Pichette was the first to testify during the procedures leading to Brother André's beatification. His role was crucial in many regards. Obviously, for the Brother, he was an indispensable confidant. For all those who never actually knew Brother André, Pichette became an invaluable source of information, as he was cognizant of every aspect of the Brother's daily life. He could even recall his friend's schedule from sunrise to sundown. Since Brother André did not keep a journal or diary, the only witness to his daily life was his longtime road companion. Pichette once said, "Every time I went to see him, I would find him reading a book about piety or meditation, or perusing one of the lives of the saints." This observation sheds new light on a man said to be virtually illiterate. It might be closer to the truth to state that Brother André simply read the books he found inspiring! Such anecdotes are more revealing than one might expect, and we are indebted to the few people who were in a position to collect them.

To let a perfect stranger share his most intimate moments, Brother André must have felt immediately a great amount of friendship, confidence, and respect for Joseph Pichette.

There was, between Pichette and Brother André, a true and constant complicity. Many of Brother André's associates or visitors also considered him a dear friend, despite the differences that might have kept them apart. This was certainly the case for Colonel George H. Ham, whose prose was quoted briefly earlier on.

The colonel was a reserve officer and worked as an advertising manager for the Canadian Pacific railroad company in Toronto. He was a very tall man: one photograph we have of him shows him towering over his friend Brother André, who seems positively dwarfed by him. Although he was a Protestant, he often visited the Oratory and carefully observed both the Brother and his work. Eventually, he decided to publish his notes in *Maclean's* magazine, where they were introduced as "the sincere opinion of a disinterested and perceptive witness." His enthusiasm was not tempered in the slightest degree by the question of religious creed. He even went so far as to write, with pious but well-intentioned exaggeration, that at the Oratory, "Probably more Protestants than Catholics have had their prayers answered."

Colonel Ham became sufficiently familiar with Brother André to write a long article about him, which he eventually made into a book. There he describes the Brother as

> a most remarkable man, and totally unpretentious at that. He considers himself merely the humble instrument of a higher power, on the behalf of which he reaches out to his fellowmen. Although he may be something of a recluse, his long years of

fasting and praying, his constant familiarity with frightful afflictions and with moral anguish of every kind have not made him morose. He measures our world with sharp insight. Cheerful, sometimes even jovial, he enjoys nothing more than a good joke. . . .

Brother André truly must have enjoyed the company of Colonel Ham. In turn, the colonel brought us precious insight into the personality of his Catholic friend, the "miracle man," as he called him. His book, which was distributed in the United States, may have helped Americans recognize the extraordinary life of the humble laborer who had worked in their factories some thirty years earlier.

Another friend who left a lasting mark on Brother André was Father André Provençal, the priest from Saint-Césaire. Unfortunately, he died in 1889, well before Brother André's exceptional influence was fully acknowledged. Thus, he never had the occasion to attest to his friend's virtues or even to describe their friendship. In fact, we know next to nothing about a relationship that may have continued well after the Brother joined his community.

One can easily imagine how much Brother André must have appreciated the man who had all but opened the college doors for him. Recall the words Father Provençal had addressed to the college authorities: "I'm sending you a saint." As his pastor, Father Provençal was quite likely to have directed the future postulant in his life of prayer and helped him to clarify his spiritual vocation. The priest must have been wholly impressed by the richness of his young friend's inner life to go to the pains of convincing him that he could indeed join a religious community, despite his obvious limitations. Perhaps Father Provençal's influence can be measured best by the fruits it bore. Brother André possessed sufficient self-confidence to carry him through the most trying times of his religious life. Most likely, he owed this self-assurance to his friend from Saint-Césaire.

Despite the trials he underwent in his early years with his congregation, Brother André never questioned his religious calling, however peculiar it may have been. The persistence with which he defended his way of doing things in an often hostile environment—at least in the beginning of his communal life—testifies to some early, powerful influence that inspired him his whole life long. Brother André must have been hard-headed indeed to do what he did for the sick, despite his brethren's carping. Again, only a very resolute man would confront his adversaries quietly, as he did, being conscious all the while of his own physical and intellectual limitations. Someone close to him must have left a lasting impression on his whole being. It is not surprising that, upon taking the religious habit, Alfred Bessette chose the name "André." He may have desired to keep with him the faithful presence of a friend whom he still needed in his daily trials.

Many, many years later, another priest became a true friend of Brother André. He was Father Emile Deguire, a fellow member of the Holy Cross Congregation. At the time, he was a young priest in his thirties and the editor of the *Saint Joseph Annals*, a monthly publication of the Oratory. During the last fifteen years of his life, Brother André used to drop in on the young cleric every evening for a friendly chat. The eighty-year-old Brother seized these occasions to share his most private thoughts with his friend.

Father Deguire died in 1988. In 1979, he was interviewed by the writer and journalist Micheline Lachance as she prepared her biography of Brother André. Certain passages of her book bear witness to the Brother's need for intimate conversations as he neared the end of his life, conversations during which he could share his faith, his suffering, and his joy. Father Deguire is quoted as saying:

> We only became true friends during the last four or five years of my stay at the Oratory. Before that, I was too shy to talk to him. He also was a very reserved person. He was a simple man. No two ways about him: he was always totally frank. He had the laugh of a child.
>
> We became close friends when the monastery where we lived was enlarged. Until then, his cell had been in the residence next to the entrance. But then he moved into a room right next to my own. Every evening, around nine-thirty or ten, there were three loud knocks on my door. I knew it was he. He would enter, lean against my rollup desk, and spend an hour talking. He never sat down. He was a born storyteller. . . .
>
> He'd talk about the sick people he had visited and the wonders accomplished by Saint Joseph. He marveled about the recoveries that he had witnessed during the day.

So it would seem that Brother André's relations with his brethren became less strained with time. Of course, his fellows did not all befriend him, but slowly, his point of view was accepted. Thus, Brother André maintained cordial and sometimes warm relations with members of his community.

It cannot be denied, though, that his peculiar attitude had often astounded and upset some of his fellows. Imagine that a poor, uneducated little Brother should receive the sick, disregard medical opinion, prescribe oil-based remedies, and, to top it off, profess total ignorance as to exactly what was happening. Such behavior was bound to provoke hostile comments and even mockery. After all, his brethren were the first witnesses of his unorthodox behavior. It is hardly surprising that it gave rise to censure and skepticism.

When Brother André's obvious sincerity had silenced even his most vociferous foes, not even they could claim, in retrospect, that he had ever caused them personal offence. He had borne their criticism and taunts as trials inherent to his mission, thereby strengthening his passionate identification with his Galilean Master's suffering. He seems to have been certain of fulfilling God's will, of having been chosen as a favored instrument of Providence, and of benefiting from Saint Joseph's protection. Such a conviction lent him serene assurance. Perhaps he knew, thanks to his discreet intelligence and innate wisdom, that those who were skeptical would one day be confounded.

FAMILIES AND FRIENDS

Just as he managed to form deep friendships within his community, Brother André befriended countless people, and entire families, from Montreal and abroad. So deep was his care for his friends that they often became his lifelong advocates. Witness the following account from Azarias Claude: "Brother André totally changed the course of my life. He taught me how to practice renunciation and how to do penance. I became a fervent disciple of Saint Joseph and received Holy Communion daily." Brother André spoke to him often of the spiritual world, to which he had introduced him. On one occasion, Azarias Claude, a shopkeeper by profession, asked him, "Brother André, don't you ever get tired of talking of these things?" The Brother countered, "Quite the contrary. I find it restful when I can converse with someone who understands me. . . . But perhaps you're tired of listening to me?"

He liked to spend time with the family of Dominique Cormier, Joseph Pichette's brother-in-law. Cormier also served as the Brother's chauffeur when he traveled throughout the city or hastened to some distant destination. Cormier would later recall, "Brother André was not averse to speeding! For example, we might leave Montreal as late as five in the afternoon, bound for Ottawa, where the Brother had to call on a dozen sick people." Before leaving, Brother André usually spent some time with the Cormier family. He loved their children and used to exclaim candidly, "It's so good to be here!"

Another of his close friends was Jules-Aimé Maucotel, the aforementioned registrar of the City of Montreal. The man had been also an organist, a cantor, a beadle, had collected money in church and even had sold candles—among other occupations. Brother André called him his counselor. Once, on a pilgrimage to the famous shrine of Sainte-Anne-de-Beaupré, near Quebec City, Maucotel said to his traveling companion, "One day, you'll see, the Oratory will be as great a place as this!"

Brother André replied, "Impossible! How could that be . . ." However, a witness to the exchange noticed that "the smile on Brother André's face revealed how secretly pleased he was. . . ." Brother André listened to his friends, just as they influenced him: they shared his dream, and voiced clearly the aspirations that were perhaps the stuff of his prayers.

The head fireman of the City of Montreal was also one of Brother André's friends; soon the Brother could count on the assistance of a fleet of Montreal firefighters.

There were many, many more friends: people from all walks of life, who, over the years, assisted Brother André in one way or another. So many that, for want of space, they all cannot be listed here.

However, one of Brother André's supporters, Joseph Malenfant, must not be forgotten in these pages: the story of his life is both strange and marvelous. In 1914, Joseph Malenfant lost his wife. His children, too, had passed away, with the exception of just one, who lived in a distant city. He was thus alone, totally. One night, in a dream, he saw an old man building a church and pleading for his help. Mr. Malenfant sold his farm and set off for Montreal with only a few belongings and with no idea of what fate held in store for him. Once in Montreal, he went to the Oratory and met Brother André, whom he instantly recognized as the old man of his dream.

He was convinced that his fate had been sealed thereby and asked to speak to the college Superior. He asked him if he might join the congregation. To this end, he could only plead, "Not to be useful to anyone means to become useless oneself!" Due to his advanced age, his request was turned down. The good man went back on the road, no less resolved to help Brother André build his church.

He traveled throughout all the eastern part of the country, from the coast of Labrador to the Province of New Brunswick. Everywhere, in each parish, he would ask for money for his cause, each time repeating the words first addressed to the college Superior: "Not to be useful to anyone means to become useless oneself!" He was quite successful. On his next visit to the Oratory, he handed Brother André the sum of $409.

Malenfant took to the road again, but this time, rather than begging for money, he sold subscriptions to the *Oratory Annals*. This he did for years, right up to his death. As he journeyed, he prayed and he solicited official endorsements. To those people kind enough to spare him a minute's attention, he would repeat his maxim: "Not to be useful to anyone means to become useless oneself!" Since he did not know how to write, he used to memorize the names of people who bought subscriptions. Each evening, he asked his hosts to inscribe those names for him on a list he was preparing for the Oratory. Over a period of ten years, he collected close to thirty-five thousand subscriptions to the periodical; all this "to help Brother André build his church."

All this testimony shows that Brother André could count on his friends to help him in his mission. Their assistance was necessary at each phase. They were always there to support him. Without their help, the Oratory never would have existed. Brother André was quite aware of all that he owed to his friends. Of course, some of them felt that they owed him their life.

Even in New England, Brother André had befriended a fair number of people, whom he called on regularly.

Why did he visit those American states? Was it because of those long-gone years when he had lived there, working in the cotton mills? Or did he want to see the members of his family who had settled there? Was he expressing his gratitude to those kind-hearted people who had traveled all the way to the Oratory to see him and had never lost the hope of some day welcoming him in turn to their own villages, to their own parishes? Was he trying to find a haven of peace, far away from the bustling life he led at the Oratory? Whatever his reasons may have been, the fact remains that Brother André went on tours of small American towns about twice a year. He always received a warm greeting. His Superiors not only encouraged him to make these journeys, they required it of him!

When on tour, Brother André might travel 600 kilometers (about 370 miles) a day, sharing frugal meals with his chauffeur. Sometimes he would set out for New England and make his way to Providence, in Rhode Island. Or he might traverse New York State, up to Albany, or even go as far as New Jersey. His hosts, on these trips, were simply good people all too happy to offer his chauffeur and him shelter for the night. Sometimes he stayed at a presbytery that happened to be on his path. When this happened, the parish priest would waste no time in calling his flock to church to pray with the famous traveler. On one occasion, a priest had brought out the entire parish to meet Brother André, who was welcomed with a procession and a solemn Mass. Special prayers were even said. All this was quite imposing! When Brother André got back to Montreal, he described the event to his brethren in these terms: "When I got to that parish, they just so happened to be celebrating a great feast. . . ." He simply could not imagine that all the pomp had been in his honor.

Obviously, these trips were tiring because of the thousands of people who wanted to see him. But, occasionally, Brother André simply could spend some time with those people of whom he was particularly fond. Even though he divested himself of many things and lived only for his fellowmen, the Brother never denied that he needed those moments of human warmth and sharing.

We sometimes think of saints as disincarnate beings, whose spiritual commitment all but stifles their simple humanity. While this may have been the case with some saints, it was not true of Brother

André. Certainly, his mission was purely spiritual. Yet he yearned to share it with his friends; indeed he sought them out for his endeavor. His was an enterprise—a life, even—shared with all those willing to work toward a common goal.

CHAPTER 5

THE FRIEND
OF THE SUFFERING

FOR MANY YEARS, while still the porter of Notre-Dame College, Brother André quietly endured his colleagues' mockery. One of his fiercest critics was the college physician, Dr. Joseph-Albin Charette. For him, Brother André was little more than a pathetic charlatan, an "Old Greaser," as he delicately put it. In his opinion, the Brother not only took advantage of poor, gullible people, but also put their health at risk. Obviously, the unexpected recoveries of some college students—which even he could not explain—only fuelled his indignation against the extemporaneous healer, whose activities he denounced with unparalleled vigor. The physician was also profoundly humiliated to see people show more confidence in Brother André than in his own medical ability. Charette made not the slightest attempt to disguise his hostile feelings toward the porter.

A day came when the proud doctor's wife fell ill. She had a nasal hemorrhage that nothing could stop. Dr. Charette tried every known remedy. He even consulted some of his colleagues and brought some into his home. Nothing came of this, and the situation quickly became critical.

One day, despairing of orthodox medical treatment, Mrs. Charette asked her husband to bring Brother André to her side. For the doctor, such a request was unacceptable. First, he did not give any credence to the pseudo-therapeutic ploys of the Brother porter. Also, he had so often attacked the latter in public that it would be terribly humiliating to beg for his help now. His wife insisted. And the hemorrhage persisted. Out of love for his cherished wife, Dr. Charette finally capitulated and asked Brother André to pay her a visit.

As the two men made their way to the patient's home, Brother André said to the physician, "She will not die." He walked into Mrs. Charette's room: the bleeding stopped immediately. There was no relapse. Never again did Dr. Charette mock the one he had dubbed—until then—"Old Greaser." He realized he had witnessed an extraordinary event, beyond even the reach of science.

Similar examples of inexplicable cures were reported, thousands of times, in Brother André's lifetime. Highly competent and impartial physicians were consulted; yet there was no disputing the fact that people diagnosed as incurable suddenly were healed after a visit with Brother André. In all sorts of circles, he now was being called a "miracle-worker." All witnesses to his feats regarded them as miracles. Until the very end of his life, millions of pilgrims begged for his intercession so that their bodies, hearts, or souls might be healed. As early as 1922, Colonel Ham wrote: "It appears that, over the past ten years, expressions of gratitude have been received from at least 30,000 people who have secured assistance, either miraculously or by means more discreetly spiritual, thanks to Brother André's intercession."

What kinds of miracles? All sorts. Several accounts have come down to us, thanks to the sick themselves, or thanks to witnesses to these events, who spoke to friends, biographers, or doctors.

We know that even as a college porter, Brother André was instrumental in bringing about the recoveries of some students. We also know that so many people from the vicinity came to him for succor that he had to greet them in a tramway shelter. And we know that finally, in 1909, he was given a private office in the new visitors' pavilion beside the hillside chapel, where he received large crowds of pilgrims.

Colonel Ham's article, published in *Maclean's,* brings us further insight into the Brother's activities. The colonel claimed that, as early as 1874, Brother André had cured victims of an epidemic. And he went on to write:

> The first major miracle that brought him wider celebrity occurred in 1910. Mr. Martin Hannon, a railroad employee, had been the victim of a serious accident two years earlier. His legs and feet had been crushed by heavy marble blocks. Hannon had been unable to walk without crutches,

and it was on crutches that he went to see Brother André. The Brother rubbed the poor man's mangled limbs with holy oil and prayed over him. He then told him to throw his crutches away and pronounced him cured. Hannon did as he was told and from then on walked without even using a cane. The following day, he went to the head-office of the Montreal newspaper *La Patrie,* spoke of his miraculous recovery, and Brother André's reputation as a "miracle man" spread afar.

Colonel Ham worked for the same company as Hannon, and therefore could vouch for the authenticity of his account. By articles such as this one, Montrealers, and soon other Canadians and Americans, were kept well informed of what was happening at the Oratory. The colonel eventually became the Brother's biographer, and wrote, again in *Maclean's*: "Catholic priests are not the only witnesses to the work of the 'miracle man of Montreal.' There are also reports from some of Montreal's most influential physicians. . . ." People from all classes of society, from the smartest set to the most unsophisticated, were convinced that Brother André was instrumental in bringing about miraculous recoveries.

Was the Brother fully conscious of the wonders with which he was being credited, humble as he was? Though he had little formal schooling, he was evidently very intelligent. Still, he considered himself more the witness than the author of these extraordinary events.

One day, Father Deguire said to him, "It's odd, Brother André, sometimes you say to the sick, 'You're cured!' And it's done. Other times, you advise them to pray to Saint Joseph and to make novenas. And to others, still, you recommend rubbing themselves with medals or the oil of Saint Joseph. Or you say, 'I'll pray for you.' Why these differences from one case to another?"

Brother André answered, "When I say to someone,' Let go of your crutches,' it's because it's clear that the person will be healed."

There was a consensus—as there still is today—that Brother André did cure the sick. No consensus was ever reached as to how this came about: when asked about the reaction of witnesses to such spectacular recoveries, Father Deguire stated, "They all considered him a miracle-worker. On the other hand, such a thought never entered Brother André's mind."

But why did he resort to remedies such as oil or medals when he knew himself to be the sole instrument, the single vehicle of these recoveries? Father Deguire explained,

> He attributed the cures to the humble trust people placed in such means. He also believed many more would be healed if they persevered, out of faith, in rubbing themselves with the oil or medals. It is also quite probable that Brother André truly believed in the natural curative powers of these remedies. This gradually became a firmly established conviction of his. Perhaps he used it to blind himself to the

miracles he was performing, or perhaps
his intent was to mystify onlookers in a
similar way.

It was Brother André's novel use of oil and medals of which critics most disapproved. During the
procedures leading to the Brother's beatification,
Father Deguire was able to qualify some of the wilder
allegations that had been made in this regard. He
pointed out that quite often, there had been simply
no call for a friction. And, of course, it never was
called for in cases where women were involved.
Father Deguire himself had had some reservations
regarding the process. Once it became clear to him
that Brother André saw in it above all "a sign of
trust," he accepted it, as many others did, as a symbol
that the Brother used in all simplicity, in the fashion
of his Nazarene Master of the Gospels.

Brother André was thoroughly convinced that he
personally had nothing to do with these miracles, of
which he was only the instrument, the vessel, and the
witness. To those who "ordered" him to heal them,
he would say, "Do you give orders to your doctor
when you consult him? Ask Saint Joseph. I, personally, can't do a thing!" He even would weep when he
heard people attributing miracles to him directly. He
confided to a friend, "How can people be so foolish?
How could anyone believe that I, Brother André,
poor and ignorant as I am, might heal them, or per-
form miracles? Well, I don't. The Good Lord is the
only author of all these miracles."

In retrospect, one can understand those witnesses
who credited Brother André with uncanny spiritual
power. After all, the Brother brought about inexplicable

and extraordinary recoveries, thousands of times, his whole life long. In 1912, the archbishop of Montreal himself admitted as much when he said, pointing to a collection of canes and crutches left behind by healed pilgrims at the Oratory, "Might I say miracles are happening here? If I were to deny it, all these instruments, silent witnesses to so much suffering, would speak in my place. . . ."

HEALING WORDS

When he began to fulfill his duties as keeper of the Oratory, Brother André felt he was not doing enough for his visitors. To help him greet the faithful, he asked for the assistance of a priest, who could celebrate the Eucharist and hear confessions. The Provincial of the congregation chose Father Adolphe Clément, who, at the age of thirty-three, had abandoned his teaching career because his eyes were failing him. When he introduced himself to Brother André, he said, "They're sending you a blind man as chaplain! I can't even read my breviary." To which Brother André answered, "Tomorrow, you'll get back to reading your breviary." And in fact, the next day, Father Clément was able to read his daily prayers again. His oculists never changed their initial diagnostic, though, and kept on reminding him, "But you can't read . . . in fact you're blind!" He stayed at the Oratory for more than twenty-five years, never had any trouble with his eyesight, and retained his dubious status as a medical enigma.

The Oratory is a house of prayer. It was therefore quite normal for Brother André to ask his visitors to go to confession, to receive Communion, to do penance, and to pray to Saint Joseph. Before healing the body, Brother André sought to convert the soul. Then again, sometimes a cure led naturally to a conversion. From the pilgrims, he expected an act of faith, or at least a sign of trust. He wanted to touch the heart while healing the body. Hence his recommendation to use, as a sign of faith, Saint Joseph's oil or a medal of the saint. He truly believed in the power of the saint to whom he prayed along with the sick. He did not always demand prayer or devotion from his callers because he knew that these would be the necessary result of a blessing. But he occasionally gave his visitors this counsel: "Hold a medal of Saint Joseph in your hand when you have a special request to make or an important transaction to conclude. . .Holding a medal in your hand, rather than just wearing it on you, reminds you of the power of Saint Joseph. It also shows greater trust in him."

Brother André himself, with personal amazement, shared with his friends stories of cures, just as a bewildered onlooker might do. He told this story, for example:

> A man who was wounded while hunting came to my office. The lead shot buried in his flesh had poisoned it, and the doctors said his hand had to be amputated. I rubbed it with Saint Joseph's oil. The poisoned flesh dripped to the ground like melting grease. My hands were covered with it. He left perfectly cured. . . .

On other occasions, Brother André brought about a recovery simply by uttering a few words—not so much by ordering the sickness to leave the body, but rather by inviting the sick person to hope against all hope.

The following story offers a good example of this, just as it silently points to the limits of science. A young physician, from one of the best hospitals in Montreal, was crippled by phlebitis; he could walk only with the help of crutches. His colleagues, all specialists in their field, were convinced that he would be handicapped for the rest of his days. A friend suggested that he consult Brother André. The young man could barely walk. Still, he made his way to the healer.

Upon seeing him, Brother André said, "You're a doctor. Have faith. Saint Joseph won't let you lose such a bright future, nor will he disregard the sacrifices your parents have made. Let go of your crutches and walk to that door." The doctor obeyed without giving it a second thought. He marched to the door once, twice, then went back and forth. Finally, Brother André said to him, "Now, leave those crutches at the Oratory, and thank Saint Joseph for having obtained such a blessing for you."

There are thousands of such canes and crutches left behind at the Oratory, still witnesses to recoveries induced by a few words, a prayer, an act of faith, or a moment of trust—in the eyes of believers, quiet proof of miracles.

Sometimes, even when dealing with an emergency, Brother André seemed to know that only a long, tortuous process would lead to recovery. Here is an account of one such case, which we owe to both the patient and Brother André:

A man in his forties suffered from a fracture of the spine at the level of the kidneys. He had to wear a metallic corset. Brother André sent for him and asked him to remove the surgical corset so that he could observe the fracture and broken vertebrae. He began by cleansing the patient's wounds and removing a large amount of pus. Finally, he suggested that the sick man stop wearing the corset. It must be mentioned here that occasionally Brother André would settle the sick on one of the two couches in his own room, for as long as he thought necessary. The man concerned stayed for over two weeks. After the first treatment, he already felt slightly better. Brother André came by to wash the wounds and rub them with oil several times a day. The ailing man slowly regained his strength, as his spine healed.

Finally, after two to three weeks of treatment, the man could walk and, eventually, he went back to work. The physicians who had treated him for years had considered this man incurable. Some had even said, "If Brother André heals him, it will be truly a miracle. . . ."

There are hundreds of similar stories. One need not recount them all to state the obvious: Brother André—especially when he was the keeper of the Oratory—met thousands of people, to whom he brought hope and consolation and, sometimes, restored health. Some of his cures have been accepted as miracles, even by the Church. This is to say that they withstood even the most rigorous scientific scrutiny. Finally, even the most skeptical of men had to concede that Brother André seemed to possess a supernatural power over body and soul.

Brother André lent his own meaning to such cures. He would say, "The recoveries and favors granted at the Oratory are proof of divine goodwill, revealed by Saint Joseph's intervention." Or again, "How good the Good Lord is! The recoveries are wonderful for the persons cured, of course, but also for those who hear of them. It strengthens their faith."

This shows how conscious the Brother was of being an instrument of God's will—a mere instrument, and no more than that. We know that he considered himself bereft of any personal power, other than that of imploring Saint Joseph's intercession. Notwithstanding, he was also convinced that he had had the unique privilege of being touched by God's grace.

Pilgrims can see in the votive chapel, next to the crypt, a collection of prostheses—canes and crutches left behind by people who were healed. Originally, they all were given personally to Brother André. As they hang from the chapel walls, they bear timeless witness to the extraordinary events that unfolded at the Oratory.

Over the years, Brother André greeted hundreds of people every day. Ordinarily, each person stayed with him for only a few minutes, just long enough for the Brother to listen to a request, and to give the advice he thought the most fitting: "Pray to Saint Joseph! Rub yourself with a medal or Saint Joseph's oil. Go to receive Communion. Confide in the Good Lord! Convert yourself! Have faith. . . ."

Many came to see Brother André hoping to be relieved of physical afflictions. If they were cured, there were always friends and relatives to testify to the fact. However, many more came to the Brother with rent souls; until then alone in their grief, they could finally unburden themselves. More often than not, words of consolation, rather than a cure, were forthcoming. Such was the nature of Brother André's solace: a new meaning given to one's life, a caring presence in one's solitude, hope offered for the future. All those who met him were deeply impressed by him. They all felt the light touch of a spiritual strength so uncommon that it is usually ascribed only to saints.

During the beatification procedures, one of his former Superiors testified,

> I can state that the work done by Brother André in his office at the Oratory, for more than 25 years, was terribly demanding. He received all sorts of visitors, listened to their complaints, gave counsel to all those who sought it, prayed with many, attended a few by rubbing their wounded limbs, also reasoned with those people who expected prodigious results by teaching them the sense of Christian resignation. People revealed to him the innermost recesses of their conscience. He was at his post every day, standing for five hours in a row, despite his old age and stomach pains, which grew worse with the years. . . .

His Superiors and brethren could only acknowledge with sincere admiration the spirituality of his work.

In the world at large, people came to a simple conclusion: Brother André was a miracle-worker. Every recovery mentioned in the newspapers or on the radio was hailed instantly as a direct intervention of Providence, which had chosen, as usual, the weakest instrument to accomplish the greatest things.

MIRACLES?

All those who met Brother André considered him a living saint. It comes as no surprise, then, that many called his deeds miraculous, whether they had actually witnessed them or merely read about them in the papers. With the exception of some implacable skeptics, opinion was undivided. Brother André was indeed a saint, and his acts were miraculous. Too many inexplicable things were happening at the Oratory for their witnesses to deny their supernatural nature.

However, the Church is very slow in acknowledging as miracles any matter of extraordinary events submitted to its scrutiny, even inexplicable recoveries. Even what seems painfully obvious to the people is not immediately accepted by ecclesiastical authorities. Why is that? Perhaps this can best be explained by the following points and counterpoints.

Miracles, since they go against the laws of nature, cannot logically stem from the Creator. How and why would they fit into his creation and his design? Miracles are nature's exceptions, moments when nature undermines its own logic. A miracle not only disrupts, but also most often negates or reverses a creature's natural evolution.

To the believer who readily accepts God's dominion over this world, miracles are quite conceivable. God rules over his creation and may intervene when and as he sees fit. Most often, his motives for doing so are not of this world. A miracle, then, symbolizes or signifies a spiritual value. It is the means by which the spiritual is revealed to this world. The Gospels explain, by Jesus' example, this conception of miracles.

Jesus accomplished extraordinary feats, such as curing the sick, because he wanted simultaneously to rekindle faith and to express charity. When Jesus heals someone, he is giving a sign to the witnesses of the event. He signifies who he is: God. And he shows what he does: he loves. Miracles can be fully understood—that is, perceived as acts of God's love—only by those who believe in him. Unbelievers can see only conjuring tricks or sorry acts of magic, all more or less spectacular or comprehensible. For one has to be prepared, to be readied for the sign, in order to recognize it when it appears and to understand its meaning.

Brother André prayed so that suffering people would be freed from their ills. He did this out of the love he bore them. Like Jesus, he had compassion for the suffering. His first desire was to deliver them, to unburden them. "What tremendous pain there is in the world! I was in a good position to see that," he once said. Like Jesus, Brother André was the vessel of God's love; he revealed that love by alleviating human suffering.

As related in the Gospels, Jesus' miracles always linked the human, indeed the humane, to the Divine. They were invoked by a cry for help, expressed directly by persons in need or by others on their behalf. Thus, initially, it is love for a person that triggers divine intervention. But also, Jesus' actions are either preceded or followed by an act of faith. Miracles, being visible signs of a supernatural presence, can be accepted fully for what they are only in a context of faith. Without faith, they cannot be recognized, much less understood. A miracle is a sign directed exclusively to the faithful.

A miracle is not a right that can be claimed. It is always an exceptional and gratuitous favor. As such, true miracles were rare during Brother André's lifetime, especially when we measure their frequency against the huge number of people he welcomed at the Oratory or visited in their homes. Yet Brother André's every gesture simultaneously fortified the faith of those delivered from their woes, and bolstered the belief of witnesses to his deeds. When God speaks, he makes sure that someone will be able to understand him.

Brother André unburdened many pilgrims and sometimes changed the course of their lives. He did this in a spirit of compassion, and his practice was perceived as such. One day, a mother brought along her daughter, who was paralyzed at the hip. Brother André, knowing that the mother herself was not well, asked her, "Madam, are you here for your own sake?" To which she replied, "No, I've come on

behalf of my four-year-old daughter: she can't walk."
The Brother insisted, "But you're also in need of
Saint Joseph's help, and you'll be healed. As for your
daughter, let her stand by herself. You'll have to run
to catch up with her." A simple enough tale, which
signifies pure compassion.

Above all, it was out of love for the people around
him that Brother André listened, gave advice, and
cured.

But it is also evident that he appealed to people's
faith. He tried to make them see with their inner
eye, that is, with their soul, the intervention of God
in their lives. Faith is sometimes expressed by trust,
sometimes by action, or sometimes by doubt overcome. Brother André knew that a sign from God
could transform a life full of doubt into a life full of
faith.

On countless occasions, he said to visitors begging for help, "Put yourself in the hands of the Good
Lord. He never abandons anyone. . . ."

Once, he confided to his friend Joseph Pichette,
"Many people are not healed because of their lack
of faith or submission to God's will. Often, they
refuse to do what I ask of them. It takes a lot of faith,
you know, to rub oneself with a medal or the oil of
Saint Joseph. . . ." These words alone reveal Brother
André's total lucidity concerning his actions and the
meaning that should be ascribed to them. What he
expected most from the sick was an act of faith. All
other deeds, frictions, and the like only served as a
means for expressing one's belief.

There were thus three possible ways in which to
perceive Brother André's work.

Popular perception was probably the furthest removed from the truth. It was thought that if people witnessed miracles, then naturally the agent of those deeds had to be a miracle-worker. Need we repeat that Brother André, personally, never believed he could work miracles? Recall that those people who called him a miracle-worker, he found foolish. In fact, the only thing he could not do was to convince the public of his powerlessness, as far as miracles went. Brother André's reputation was built against his own will. He never talked much. He never solicited the media and never tried to defend his actions before large audiences; nor did he ever address forums of theological or scientific experts. These factors may have contributed to the public's misapprehension of his work. Even Colonel Ham, a self-styled "objective and lucid" biographer, referred to Brother André as the "miracle man of Montreal." Much as Brother André would have wanted to silence them, the very walls of the Oratory seemed to speak of his prowess.

Faced with such misguided admiration, Brother André always reacted in the same way. He tried to show the power of God's love for the suffering. All that was happening at the Oratory, all those tangible signs left there by the sick—canes, crutches, surgical corsets, and all matter of objects—were meant to touch the hearts of incredulous visitors. To them, Brother André could only say, "See how good the Good Lord is! How he cares for us all!"

Those who actually met the Brother, rather than simply hearing about him, often had no choice but to perceive his deeds in a fashion entirely different from that of the public at large. With these people, Brother André made little case of his rumored powers and talked only to their faith. These appeals sometimes would be formulated strangely, so that the sick might well receive startling answers to their requests. One of his companions, Bruno Ganz, recorded the words Brother André spoke to a hospitalized patient: "You'll die tomorrow. The Good Lord wants you with him. But don't worry about your family. Saint Joseph will see to everything. . . ." What the Brother hoped for— or sometimes even provoked—was, then as always, the ultimate act of faith.

To a person who was practically "ordering" Brother André to heal him, he said, "Your request will go unheeded because you do not trust in God. You're demanding a recovery, as if I were a physician. If you think God owes you something, go and ask him for it yourself!" Without faith, nothing could be obtained: indeed, who would be listening to prayers? And Brother André added, "God doesn't owe you a thing. Abandon yourself to his will."

Furthermore, Brother André never would allow acts of faith to be used in a process of bartering with God. For had he ever prayed with anything less than total disinterest for those who had asked for his intervention? To anyone saying, "If I'm cured, I'll give alms, or I promise to do such-and-such," Brother André answered, "Does God owe you anything? You cannot strike a deal with the Good Lord. Start first by giving alms or by doing whatever you promise to do. Then, if God sees fit to heal you, he'll do so!"

Finally, what were Brother André's thoughts regarding his own person? They could not have been further removed from popular rumor. He saw himself as a humble and powerless servant, capable only of presenting to Saint Joseph and to his Son the requests submitted to him.

However, Brother André was quite aware of an extraordinary power that seemed to spring from the very roots of his being. In other words, he was convinced of the force of his prayers, since they could induce Saint Joseph's intercession. But he was even more convinced that the ultimate power of healing rested only with God. Brother André listened to the suffering, commended them to Saint Joseph, and the Good Lord did the rest of the work. Only because of his total confidence in Saint Joseph was he able to show the authority he did when he healed by simply stating, "You're not sick!" For Brother André, Saint Joseph could obtain anything from his Son. All that was needed was to ask him! And that is what the Brother did. The whole process was mysterious. But Brother André had the key to it, and that key was Saint Joseph.

CHAPTER 6

SAINT JOSEPH'S FRIEND

THIS WAS SOMETHING of an obsession for Brother André. He wanted to build a chapel on the mountain, an Oratory dedicated to Saint Joseph. Why, in particular, Saint Joseph?

We know that his mother first taught little Alfred to love Saint Joseph. Azarias Claude, who heard this from Brother André, explained that as a child, Alfred often prayed with his mother. On such occasions, she would let her son's fingers run along on the beads of her rosary as she said it. The first prayer that the child memorized was the simple invocation "Jesus, Mary, Joseph." To a young mind, the three holy figures were as one. Alfred must have felt a particular affinity with the third one, Joseph. We know that he was called "Saint Joseph's fool" by the youngsters of Saint-Césaire. They would say, "He's going crazy with his devotion to Saint Joseph!" This is the first clue we have to his childhood habit of praying to Saint Joseph. His attachment to the saint was quite unusual.

Is this bond between the Brother and the saint so surprising? Not really, if we consider that both of them shared a similar mystery.

In the Gospel according to Luke, Saint Joseph is portrayed as a discreet man, conscious of the immense responsibility he must accept without quite understanding it. He trusts in God, to be sure. Still, he shows great humility in accepting the role into which he is cast. He is a faithful, silent servant, and a servant so retiring that he was almost forgotten for several centuries, even by the Church. In short, Joseph's existence is justified only by the Child he serves. He accompanies Mary, he protects his Son, he works in silence. He fulfills his mission, that of being God's most docile instrument as he reveals his love to the world. Joseph is the man forgotten when we revere those he served. Joseph stands aside to make way for those greater than he is. He works ceaselessly, and yet never a word is spoken about him. Joseph is Jesus' first friend, Mary's loving companion: a true family man, who would do anything for those he loves.

Joseph is not a doctor of the law or a scribe. He is an uneducated laborer, working with his bare hands. Joseph is an exile, struggling to survive in a foreign land. He is an ever-watchful confidant, listening and giving counsel. We go to Joseph, without being overwhelmed by awe, when we want to converse with the Mother and Child. Joseph is the mediator, the link, the bridge.

Is it so surprising that Brother André should feel close to him? Young Alfred knew, early on, that Saint Joseph could lead him to a life dedicated to his fellowmen. He knew he could put his faith in him.

In fact, Brother André was quite astute when he placed himself under Saint Joseph's protection. The saint surely would understand him, and never could abandon him. Saint Joseph, so to speak, was put on the spot. He simply had to help somebody whose life so resembled his own. The saint had to assist a person who so desired, deep in his heart, to follow his example. Once the bonds of friendship were sealed between the two, nothing could rend them apart. Saint Joseph and Brother André would become inseparable partners dedicated to the service of those seeking help.

Countless witnesses stated that Brother André incessantly encouraged pilgrims to pray to Saint Joseph. "Pray to Saint Joseph!" Or, "I'll pray to Saint Joseph for you. . . ." Some even said that nobody could talk to the Brother without hearing, at least once, the words "Saint Joseph."

Not because he spoke "of" or "about" Saint Joseph. No, that is not it. In fact, Brother André was not a great talker. All the words ascribed to him, throughout his whole life, have been set down in a book only seventy pages long! Very few words, for someone who lived to the ripe old age of ninety-one, greeted millions of visitors, and met with people from all ranks. He listened; he did not speak.

Christians, as a whole, know very little about Jesus' foster father. For centuries, he was almost forgotten. Perhaps he is best remembered in Canada.

The very year Alfred Bessette joined Notre-Dame College, in 1870, the Vatican officially chose Saint Joseph as the patron saint of Canada. For the young Brother, the coincidence may have been striking.

At the outset, Brother André was not aware of having a special mission to fulfill within the Church. But he had found his goal in life: he would promulgate the devotion to Saint Joseph; he would spread word of the saint's power and affection. All of Brother André's actions, up to his death, expressed his total confidence in Saint Joseph as well as his devotion to the great saint, his friend.

Witnesses, time and time again, reported Brother André's most usual advice. "He recommended very simple prayers, such as 'Saint Joseph, pray for me as you yourself would have prayed, had you been here on earth, in my shoes, with my troubles. Saint Joseph, answer our prayers. . . .'" Or Brother André would say, "Go and pray in front of the statue of Saint Joseph, and tell him, 'If you were in my place, is there nothing you would want done for you? Well, do just that for me. . . .'" Again, he might recommend this prayer: "Saint Joseph, as you can see, I'm the head of a large family. Help me as you would have liked to be helped yourself, had you been here on earth in my situation. . . ."

In fact, Brother André directly involved Saint Joseph in his affairs. He compelled the saint to react! This he did, in a rather spectacular fashion, when he met Mgr. Joseph Hallé, the vicar apostolic of Northern Ontario. The vicar himself recounted the story:

> Once, while on a trip to Saint Joseph's sanctuary, I met that dear Brother André.

During our conversation, I mentioned that I had undertaken my pilgrimage in order to commend to Saint Joseph not only my vicarship, but also, in particular, a boarding school in Hearst which bore the saint's name.

"How much do you owe on that house?" asked Brother André.

"A fair amount: 25,000 dollars."

"And you say that the school's patron saint is Saint Joseph?"

"Yes, that's so," I answered.

"Well, put up a sign in the school chapel, saying, 'Saint Joseph, pay your bills!'"

I argued, "Shouldn't I be a little more ceremonious in the choice of words?"

"Not at all!" said Brother André.

Back in Hearst, I did put up a sign, formulated in a somewhat more gracious manner. It read, "Good Saint Joseph, please pay the amount owed on your boarding school."

We all prayed to that end for three years, the nuns, the schoolchildren, and some of the faithful. The incriminating notice was left beneath the statue of Saint Joseph all that time. But the saint did not seem unduly affected by it. I now understand that he was biding his time, waiting for us to put a little of our own into this blessing we asked of him.

The favor was indeed forthcoming. It was finally granted. I cannot publicly say how it came about. Suffice it to say, to Saint Joseph's greater glory, that it came from the source least expected. Saint Joseph's

protection seemed all the more evident and
admirable. . . .

THE MEDAL
AND THE OIL

Brother André wanted to show his trust in Saint
Joseph through simple, tangible signs, signs that
some onlookers might even find mundane. One of
these signs was the saint's medal, which he gave to
all his visitors.

He always carried several medals on him. As one
witness remembered, "He invariably reached into his
pocket for medals of Saint Joseph, which he handed
out left and right. He insisted particularly on prayer
to Saint Joseph." For the one did not go without the
other. Yes, he did recommend wearing the medal,
but his advice also was to talk to Saint Joseph—in
the simplest of prayers. On one occasion, he said to
a nun, "Hold a medal of Saint Joseph in your hand
whenever you must deal with other people. If it's
possible, send them a medal of Saint Joseph before
your meeting. Pray to Saint Joseph. I'll pray along
with you, and everything will work out fine."

There are numerous records of extraordinary
events associated with Saint Joseph's medal. For
example, in a letter sent to the Oratory in 1925, one
mother related the story of her little girl, who was
crippled with infantile paralysis.

The child's parents had made a novena and had
prayed to Saint Joseph constantly. One day, they
brought their three-year-old child to the Oratory.
They prayed with all their hearts, and made their

little girl, Jacqueline, kiss a medal of Saint Joseph. All of a sudden, little Jacqueline started walking. "Since then," wrote the mother, "she runs around all day. . . ."

The medal might simply supplement the faithful's prayers; on occasion, it could also become the instrument of wondrous events. Not just the medal, though. Brother André also used another sign, to which he gave great importance: an oil that he attributed to Saint Joseph, and to which he gave the saint's name. He called it "Saint Joseph's oil." Why the use of such an oil? Where did he get such an idea? To what did he attribute its power? These questions are worthy of serious investigation.

In the Old Testament, priests anointed kings and prophets with oil. Thus, the use of oil bore a special meaning, that of heralding royalty or of conferring gifts of prophecy. In the New Testament, the Epistle of Saint James mentions a "holy" oil used to anoint the sick, for the good of their souls if not their bodies. These traditions are still alive in some of the sacraments of the Roman Catholic Church: baptism, confirmation, holy orders, and the anointing of the sick. Thus, one traditionally imputes to holy oil a portentous power, that of linking the Divine Presence to important liturgical acts and to the people affected by them.

Brother André may have been aware of these practices. But it is far from certain that biblical or sacramental tradition had anything to do with the Brother's selection, as a favored sign, of an oil he associated personally with Saint Joseph. Thanks to Canon Catta, we know of a devotion practiced during the nineteenth century at the oratory of the French city of Tours. There, the faithful burnt oil in front of a picture of Christ; soon the oil was claimed to be instrumental in curing the sick. The founder of this sanctuary, a saintly man by the name of Joseph Dupont, happened to be a close friend of Basile Moreau, the founder of the Holy Cross Congregation.

At about the same time, two short books were published in France: the first in 1864, and the second in 1874. Their aim was to encourage the devotion to Saint Joseph, as "patron and model for the soul" and as "advocate for desperate causes." In the accounts of recoveries deemed miraculous, the use of an oil burnt in front of Saint Joseph's statue was mentioned. It is possible that Brother André got wind of these cures and heard about the oil to which they were credited by way of Saint Joseph's intercession.

But it is more likely that the young postulant, while still a porter at his college, was inspired by contemporary literature. Indeed, at the time, some members of the Holy Cross Congregation—who had settled in Neuilly, France—were circulating articles from the *Annals of the Saint Joseph Association*. Canon Catta, in particular, drew from the *Annals* "the account of two cases in which unfortunate patients were the object of a 'wondrous cure.' The affected parts of their bodies were anointed with a little oil. No ordinary oil, though. After two or three novenas, it had been burnt before a relic, or a statue of Saint Joseph. One will note, also, a singular form of piety practiced in an Italian convent. There, the chapel is kept ablaze with lamps and candles burning in front of the saint's altar, the better to illuminate the words inscribed there: 'Saint Joseph has rewarded his servants a thousand times over for their faith.'"

If Brother André heard about these marvelous stories, he may have been convinced easily that oil burning in front of a statue of Saint Joseph, whom he loved so much, could indeed become a sign of that saint's compassion. The oil had no special power as such. Yet it induced an act of trust: its simple use was infused with extraordinary meaning.

Above all, Brother André wanted to lead people to prayer, to conversion, and, ultimately, to faith. He never tired of repeating, "Pray to Saint Joseph. He'll never leave you out in the cold." Or again, "Saint Joseph's ascendancy over the heart of God and that of his Holy Mother, the Virgin Mary, is beyond doubt." And even, "You must always pray to Saint Joseph. Not only when you're sick. That's not enough. You have to pray to him all the time."

However, this never deterred Brother André from using, as often as necessary, Saint Joseph's oil as a favored means of healing. Nothing could better illustrate this point than the following tale, related in a letter received at the Oratory in 1925. A mechanic had been seriously injured at work. The young man, a factory worker, had been holding in his hands a bowl of molten lead when it had exploded and burnt his whole face. The petroleum jelly applied to his charred skin did little to relieve the pain, and his eyes were so badly burnt that it was feared he would become blind. In this case, Brother André simply "added" some oil of Saint Joseph to the remedies prescribed to the young man. Here, then, is an excerpt from the mechanic's letter:

The Sunday after my accident, I asked my fiancée to come with me to the Oratory. By the way, it was freezing the day I set out. People tried to dissuade me from going, but to no avail.

When I arrived at the Oratory, I asked to see Brother André. I was told, "Brother André is at the monastery having his breakfast." I was not discouraged; I simply went to ring at the monastery door. Reverend Father Deguire was appalled when he saw my face. I asked to see Brother André. It seems that there were formal orders not to disturb him. I pleaded with Father Deguire, even argued a bit. Finally the good Brother André showed up at the end of the hallway, and asked what was going on. I said to him, "Brother André, as you can see, I'm much too young to lose my eyesight. . . . You surely can do something for me." Brother André answered, and I'm writing down the exact words of his reply, "Who says you're going to lose your eyesight? You have faith in Saint Joseph? Well then, go to church, attend Mass, and receive Holy Communion in honor of Saint Joseph. Keep on taking your medication, add to it a drop of Saint Joseph's oil, and make the following invocation: 'Saint Joseph, pray for us.' All will go well. Good day! Have faith. . . ."

I did exactly as I had been told, and after Mass, I took a little snack in a restaurant. The waitress was moved to tears when she saw me.

To sum up, let me just say this: the same evening, my fiancée applied my medication with some of the oil, and we recited the invocation in honor of Saint Joseph. The next day—oh! How wonderful!—the scars on my face peeled away like sheets of cellophane paper. My eyelids were completely healed. My face was as fine as could be. No scars left, no pain whatsoever. . . .

Another anecdote reveals the meaning that Brother André lent to the use of the oil. Brother Rosario, of the Holy Cross Congregation, confided to his now famous colleague that he was suffering from mastoiditis. Already five doctors had refused to operate on him because the risks involved were too great. Brother André said to him, "Use Saint Joseph's oil." This was done, but in vain. Brother Rosario returned to the Oratory, where Brother André simply reiterated his first counsel. Brother Rosario then said, "If you could just touch me, I believe I would have faith. . . ."

"Never! The others would think it was my doing. . . ." Finally, Brother Rosario was cured. And Brother André had made him understand the meaning he attributed to the oil. It was meant to lead to Saint Joseph and not to his humble servant.

One thing is certain: Brother André was convinced of the curative virtues, not just of the oil, but of the oleaginous friction itself. Joseph Pichette left us this account: "He rubbed people with oil to cure them and, sometimes, even after a long and hard day, this could last for more than an hour. In the case of one sick person, the treatment lasted for more than three weeks."

"These frictions were always accompanied and followed by prayers to Saint Joseph," explained Father Cousineau, Brother André's Superior, and a frequent witness of this peculiar treatment. Being modest, even scrupulous, as were so many clerics of the time, Brother André never rubbed the patient's skin itself. Actually, he would knead a man through his clothes. So convinced was he of the therapeutic nature of these frictions that he used to ask his brethren to attend him in the same fashion when his stomach caused him too much pain. And he said this relieved him.

Some faithful stated after the fact, "He said he asked us to rub ourselves lengthily because this constituted an act of love and of faith, of trust and humility." Brother André himself commented, "Many more people would be cured if they only persevered in such frictions." Such a statement testifies to his faith in the "treatment" itself. It must have been a potent sign indeed!

Brother André talked very little about the true causes underlying the recoveries of which he was the instrument. Therefore, we cannot know with certainty his innermost thoughts on the subject. Quite probably, though, he used medals and oil much as Jesus had used earth and mud to cure the sick. Brother André hid behind such signs because he did not want to be personally credited with the recoveries; nor did he wish to be thereby labeled a miracleworker. At the end of his life, he confided to a Sister attending him, "If people only knew what it truly means when I ask them to rub themselves with the medal of Saint Joseph. . . ."

Earlier on in these pages, mention was made of the reactions of both clerics and scientists to such peculiar remedies. Brother André was mocked by his fellows as a young Brother, and, with some exceptions, ridiculed by physicians during his entire life. There were some doubts concerning his possible neglect of hygienic precautions in the treatment of open or infected wounds. It must be understood that in these cases, without proper aseptic measures, diseases can be spread easily by touch. And what would happen should a patient interrupt his prescribed therapy, after one of the Brother's "bogus cures," as they were sometimes called? Families or physicians might well file lawsuits. Thus Brother André's care of the sick could have had dire consequences; his own reputation, that of his community, and that of the Church itself could have been sullied.

Ever cautious, Brother André never advised a patient to stop seeing his physician. In certain circumstances, he would even say, "Go to a doctor, who knows what may come of it." But often, people were cured before even having time to see a doctor. He also stated, in cases where surgery was recommended, "I understand surgery can be necessary, but I believe that some doctors make hurried decisions where amputation or operations are concerned."

On a few occasions, however, his advice was audacious, and even showed some temerity. Witness the account of a twenty-eight-year-old man, whose leg had to be amputated because gangrene had set in. On the eve of the amputation, Brother André went

109

to the young man's side. In tears, the patient showed him his leg, which had turned blue due to necrosis. Brother André said to him, "I bet you don't like it one bit to have your leg cut off! Well! It won't be necessary. Tomorrow, pay your hospital bill. Take these medals of Saint Joseph, and get some of his oil. Go home and rub your leg with the medals and oil. Saint Joseph will cure you." The patient did exactly as he was told, to the utter desperation of his physician. Five weeks later, the young man was at the Oratory to show his healed leg to Brother André.

The Brother never lost the support of his Superiors from the college, the Oratory, or the archbishopric; on several occasions, they even rallied to his defense. Nor was he ever sued for unwittingly harming a patient. This goes to show that he exercised not just spiritual, but also human caution. It could be said that he put both prudence and prayer on his side. Actually, some of his friends were doctors, such as Doctor Lamy, who was his physician for years. In fact, Brother André cured the latter of diphtheria. A few days later, when Dr. Lamy had recovered fully, he found the following note under his plate: "What do you think of a physician cured by a charlatan?"

Brother André used to say to those few doctors who dared be seen conversing with him, "Yours is a beautiful science, and it's God's gift to you. You must therefore be grateful and pray to Him."

A GRATUITOUS GIFT

Recoveries, however spectacular, are not necessarily miraculous. During the beatification procedures, as is required by ecclesiastical process, a few cases of healing were admitted as evidence. Because they could not be explained scientifically, they were acknowledged as miraculous acts. In other words, they were judged to be the result of divine intervention in this world.

Obviously—and this is as true today as ever—miracles refer to the faith of their witness. This frame of reference, of course, is not a universal one. Furthermore, although the science of the day may be powerless to explain certain phenomena, one can assume that future scientific developments might well shed new light on them. Clearly, science can only reach as far as permits its present state of research.

Also, certain recoveries can be explained by purely human factors, such as psychological ones. There were no systematic analyses of all the recoveries that occurred at the Oratory. People witnessed wonderful events, and the persons concerned simply thanked Brother André for his deeds. Yet illnesses are not necessarily of a physical nature. Brother André exercised an immense power of persuasion that, on occasion, may have influenced the psychological behavior of a person thought to be physically ill.

It would be a grave error, also, to assess the Brother's work only in the light of spectacular healing, be it miraculous or not. His influence was often very discreet, but no less tangible or effective—albeit in a different realm—than are wondrous cures.

Undoubtedly, he did show a marked affection for the sick. During the procedures leading to his beatification, one witness came forward with this portrait of him: "Brother André spent his whole life caring for his neighbor. He befriended everyone. People shared their worries with him. He particularly loved the poor, and he never took into consideration matters of religious belief or ethnic origin." This testimony is far from being exceptional. Brother André was known as "the Good Samaritan of Mount Royal." He was especially attentive to the needs of the poor, be they sick or not; he sought to attend them in any way possible. His friend Arthur Ganz never forgot the following incident, which affords ample evidence of the Brother's love for the poor:

> One day, I went along with him to visit a very poor family. Wooden boxes, turned upside down, served as tables and chairs. Brother André comforted the mother, saying he'd pray for her four sick children. He assured her that they would feel better by the next day. When Brother André was about to take his leave, the mother tried to give him 50 cents.
>
> He refused to accept the money, saying, "It's unacceptable, Madam, to do such a thing. You lack everything, and you want to give me alms!"
>
> Out of the house, Brother André said to me, "We've got to help this poor family." We paid a visit to one of his friends, who took it upon himself to have supplies sent to the family. We went back to see them two days later. The children were well and running about!

He accepted money from the poor only when he knew his refusal would humiliate them. According to

Br. André as a novice, ca. 1871. When Alfred Bessette entered the novitiate on December 27, 1870, he was twenty-five years old.

The Collége Notre-Dame du Sacré Cœr was founded in 1869 by the Congregation of Holy Cross. This picture of the college was taken in 1875.

Br. André wanted to build a chapel facing the college where the faithful could come to pray to St. Joseph. This first chapel was built in 1904. The small, white-haired figure at right is said to be Br. André.

A newer, larger chapel was built in 1908. A sacristy and steeple were added in 1910. This is a view of the chapel in 1915.

Br. André was one of a group of delegates who attended the Congregation of Holy Cross' General Chapter at the University of Notre Dame in 1920. He is in the center of the group.

Br. André with Col. George H. Ham, friend and author of a 1922 biography on Br. André, *The Miracle Man of Montreal*. This picture was taken in 1921.

Azarias Claude, "He would put that money aside to have Masses said for the poor." Also, he would give more of his time to the poor who came to see him in his office. He claimed that rich people had little time to spare, while the poor had more time on their hands. Perhaps, on such occasions, he was thinking of his own youth, or of his own family.

He would not have visited the poor so often simply to rid them of their ailments. Had that been his goal, one visit surely would have sufficed! He offered them a little solace and, on occasion, some advice as to how to carry on their lives, counsel garnered from his years of experience as their trusted confidant. For instance, to a couple who had already been on better terms, he said, "Household quarrels are like drafts. To create a draft, you need to open two windows. Close one, and you stop the draft. By the same token, Madam, if you stop responding to your husband's taunts, eventually he will shut up!"

He always tried to bring people closer to the Lord, and he was disappointed often. He once said, "It's odd. . . . I'm often asked for cures, but very rarely for the virtue of humility or the spirit of faith. And they're so important!" He asked people to pray, to fast, and to do penance. He greeted sinners by bidding them to go to confession. Above all, he welcomed all those who came to him with defeated souls, seeking nothing more than hope.

Millions of people visited the Oratory. Relatively few were cured of actual physical ailments. Why, then, go there? Why a pilgrimage or a visit to the Oratory? Often, simply to meet a saint, a man of prayer, a man of faith. Often, also, to allay one's sadness, grief, sorrow, or distress. Sometimes, to rekindle the will or the strength to live. Some went on their own behalf; many more traveled on behalf of their loved ones. About the solace found at the Oratory, none whispered a word. Nothing, in fact, would be known about it, had there not been the occasional confidence or discreet allusion. Pilgrims went to meet somebody, in his office up there on the mountain. They talked with him; they came away convinced that they had received a blessing. Brother André lived only for those people. As to him, he was quite content to be nothing more than "Saint Joseph's little dog," as he put it.

CHAPTER 7

THE MAN BEHIND
THE NAME

THE FIRST FRENCH settlers in Canada were a proud people; the same could be said of the Bessette family. Canon Catta drew up Brother André's genealogical tree, mapping his ancestry all the way back to those pioneers who ventured boldly to France's North American colony, New France.

France had decided that the best way to defend its colony was to implement an aggressive population policy. To this effect, it was not sufficient merely to defend the cities of Quebec and Ville-Marie, as Montreal was first named, against the attacks of the "savages." In times of truce, France tried to extend its dominion over its colony's bountiful untamed lands. Thus, in 1672, Jean Talon, the administrator of New France, distributed lands to the most deserving settlers, in accordance with "the good pleasure of the King." In particular, on October 29, 1672, M. de Chambly, captain of the famous Carignan Regiment, was granted a lord's estate, a "seigniory," as those lands were called. His grounds lay around the fort that already bore his name. Seventeen pioneers accompanied their lord to clear the land; among them was a certain Jean Bessin. On October 14, 1673, Bessin's lord, M. de Chambly, officially endowed him with a plot of farmland.

Bessin came from the town of Cahors, situated in a region of southern-central France known as Quercy. There, it is said, the people are as strong as their ink-colored wine. Jean Bessin's true name was Jean Bessède, according to his wedding certificate.

However, in New France, he lived among settlers hailing from northwestern France, particularly from the provinces of Normandy and Perche. In those parts, only the surname "Besset," and some minor variants, were familiar. This explains how the pioneer's name from "Bessin" slipped to "Besset." And it was only a matter of time before the last consonant was doubled to match the pronunciation of the word. So the spelling of the name, from Bessin, through Bessède and Besset, finally settled as Bessette. Our pioneer was the ancestor of all the Bessettes of Canada and America.

There is an anecdote that offers some insight into Besset's character. On the very day he joined his regiment, he was nicknamed *"Brisetout,"* which can be rendered in English as "Rough and Tough." He must have been a fiery and bold fellow! Actually, this should not come as a surprise: the timid rarely became soldiers in faraway Canada, and only the intrepid would think of settling the snowy wilderness.

His wife, Anne Le Seigneur, was perhaps one of those young women known as the *Filles du Roy*— literally, the "King's daughters." These girls, most often the orphaned daughters of the king's soldiers, had been taken in charge by the French State; eventually, hundreds were brought to New France, there to find a husband and to populate the colony. It was expected of these founding women that they be courageous and healthy, but also, inasmuch as was possible, untainted by "repelling features." Peter Kalm, a Swedish historian who visited New France, wrote: "The women of Canada are hardworking, especially among the lower classes. . . . They work in the fields, the prairies, and the stables. No labor is too hard for them. . . ." This, then, is the portrait of the first maternal ancestor: a brave and worthy woman. She would have worked the land with her husband, and together they would have adopted the hard life of a farmer.

The Bessets, like so many of their countrymen, had many children. And why not? The handsome sum of £300 was awarded to families with ten children and more. The first son was named after his father: Jean Besset. In 1695, he married Marie-Anne Benoît, who bore him a little girl.

Life was far from easy. The Iroquois were always on the attack, destroying harvests and slaughtering livestock, if not pioneers. In 1689, there was a massacre at Lachine, and there were fierce battles in the whole region south of Montreal. The Bessets lived in the valley of the Richelieu River, a favorite target of Iroquois raids. On August 9, 1697, Marie-Anne Besset was killed during one of these attacks. Legend has it that her husband Jean, scalped as he had been, battled on. This does appear somewhat odd, since victims of this harsh custom seldom survived.

Be that as it may, Jean Besset not only survived but also remarried in 1700. His second wife, Madeleine Plamondon, bore him four daughters and three sons: quite a large family, when one considers the three children of Besset's first marriage. The eldest son, Jean, became a soldier. The second son, Jean-François, followed his elder brother into the Army, and together they served in what is now Northern Ontario. There Jean-François married his captain's daughter. He must have loved her madly: their first child was born out of wedlock.

In 1750, soon after the couple's return to the family farm in Chambly, the young bride died. Jean-François Besset bore his grief by taking a second wife, Marie-Joseph Girard. She bore him many children.

Among them was a son named Joseph, born in 1753. Now some years later, in 1779, Joseph was blessed in turn with a son, to whom he gave the name of Joseph. In 1799, the latter married Marie-Josephte Cyr, and four years later they baptized their son Joseph. After the death of his wife and son, Joseph Besset remarried, this time with Angélique Laporte, on August 8, 1803. Their firstborn received the name Joseph, and the third son was baptized Isaac. So finally we meet Alfred's father: it is he, Isaac Bessette, born on February 13, 1807. Twenty-four years later, on September 27, 1831, he married Clothilde Foisy, a sweet girl just seventeen years old. And she is the one who used to settle little Alfred on her lap and teach him to pray; it is she, also, who told her son everything there was to know about the patron saint of all those ancestors called Joseph.

In the early part of the nineteenth century, the wars with the Iroquois were things of the past. This is not to say that these were peaceful years. In the Richelieu River valley, where Isaac Bessette and his family lived, many men were "Patriots," that is, established French settlers who only grudgingly accepted British rule—even though this dominion had begun years before, in 1763. Their discontent was aimed not at history, though, but at the recent changes sweeping the land. The English presence was becoming increasingly overwhelming. Old French families were displaced by new English settlers. Many of these came from the Canadian West and settled in villages in the southeastern region of Montreal. Soon English strongholds sprung up throughout the area.

The original French-Canadian settlers felt betrayed by recent changes in legislation and land allotment. They eventually formed organizations to voice their discontent. At first, they circulated manifestos and sent lists of grievances to the British government in London. When words no longer sufficed, the "Patriots" took up arms. By the fall of 1837, the British had a full-fledged rebellion on their hands.

The battles were fought along the Richelieu River. The "Patriots" won a few skirmishes before being violently put down. Those insurgents who had not perished were made prisoners by the English. Some were hanged; others, deported. Their hopes crushed, the people of the Richelieu valley returned to their lands and to their tools. They were unsettled and anxious. In 1840, in this valley where Clothilde and Isaac Bessette dwelt, life seemed less than glorious and the future less than promising. One had to be truly courageous, and to respect deeply the gift of life, to go on bearing children and trusting in the future. In fact, people needed the faith and hope their ancestors had carried with them from the Old World some two hundred years earlier.

Clothilde Foisy lacked neither faith nor hope. Her ancestor, Martin Foisy, had set foot in New France a few years before the arrival of her husband's ancestors. This was in 1643, one year after the foundation of Ville-Marie. Martin Foisy established himself in Cap-de-la-Madeleine, near Trois-Rivières, halfway between Quebec City and Montreal. Certain historians claim he was related to Louis Hébert, the first colonist to work the land in Canada. Some of Clothilde's distant relatives belonged to the self-styled nobility of the time, such as Jean Le Gras, Jacques de la Porte, and even Marguerite de la Jemmerais, Lady of Youville, the founder of the Gray Nuns. Eventually, Martin Foisy's progeny settled on the lands near Chambly. It is said that they were all well educated: as early as 1800, every Foisy could sign his own name, not a small feat in those days.

Some of them were millers. A certain Claude Foisy, a baker, married Ursule Barsalou, who gave birth to eight children, and named her sixth child Clothilde. Clothilde, in turn, married Isaac Bessette in 1831, well before the "troubles" began between long-established French settlers and recent English colonists. In 1845, she gave birth to Alfred, who eventually would be known the world over by the name of Brother André.

THE LIFE OF THE POOR

The first colonists of New France had led lives fraught with danger and difficulty. Their descendants also struggled to live. Among those pioneers there were surely many unsung heroes. Of course, people living in the cities could hope to acquire, little by little, certain advantages: some degree of comfort in their homes, better supplies of food and other necessities, and some access to the world at large. Most of all, they could hope, within reason, to get richer. Not so for the peasants in the countryside. For them, working the land meant backbreaking labor, shabby housing, and ridiculously small wages. Large houses were for the big landowners, the lords. Farmers lived in small one- or two-room houses, at a time when large families were the rule rather than the exception. One can only wonder at the harmony that existed in most of these homes in circumstances so trying.

Isaac Bessette knew of no other life than that of the poor, and all he could bequeath to his family was that hard-earned knowledge.

Even tranquility was beyond the reach of the poor, in those lands so close to the American border. Loyalists arrived there in droves, fleeing the American Revolution, as did newly endowed English settlers. Even the old seigniories were dismantled, giving way to townships. All this unsettled entire families who, having never owned much of anything, had never learned to defend what little was theirs. Alfred was four years old when his father left Saint-Grégoire to practice his trade as a carpenter in Farnham. Farnham was the first of those newborn "English" towns populated in majority by that second wave of colonists, progressing sometimes from the South, sometimes from the North, to take over lands originally claimed by French pioneers.

From early on in their childhood, the Bessette children had to adapt to an environment foreign, if not hostile, to them. For in Farnham, as elsewhere throughout the country, relations were strained between the two linguistic communities. In those days, the French-speaking people were known as the "Canadians," and the others were simply called the "English"—as they sometimes still are today. In Farnham, English-speaking people formed the biggest and the wealthiest part of the population. The English were masters; the French Canadians, servants. The socioeconomic context was hardly favorable to the fashioning of exuberant personalities. It comes as no surprise that Isaac Bessette was said to be taciturn. Equally unsurprising is the fact that the same was said of Brother André. It was not so much a question of education or upbringing. Such an environment and the lifestyle it bred were bound to mold introspective, if not withdrawn, characters. But retiring as they were, those people were strong-willed and armed with a determination that nothing could break.

Faced with common hardship, they developed—out of necessity—a strong spirit of solidarity, particularly manifest within families. Recall that the large families of the time had to share very limited living quarters. In these homes, nothing ever belonged to a single individual, since everything had to be shared with eight to ten relatives. Joyful occasions also were a family affair. Aunts, uncles, and cousins would congregate to celebrate feast days, holidays, or simply to mark days of good cheer. People made do with simple, quiet pleasures. In short, what moments of happiness people enjoyed were shared with their family, which explains why their first concern was always for the wellbeing of their kith and kin.

The wellbeing of kith and kin; one can easily imagine the helpless rage of the poor as they watched friends and relatives suffer the onslaughts of dreadful diseases. Child mortality was high, and only a high birthrate could balance the ravages of illness or epidemics. People learned to live with sickness and death as constant companions. When people came to Brother André in the last years of his life, asking him to share with them the secret to a long life, he used to say, "Work as much as possible and eat as little as possible." Of course, that was what he had done his whole life long. It was also a way of life he had witnessed throughout his childhood and youth.

With so few doctors and even fewer hospitals in the countryside, what could people do but desperately pray for some kind of reprieve from illness? Brother André surely remembered such desperate scenes from his childhood, when his kin became the helpless witnesses or the forceless victims of some merciless disease. The only recourse was a prayer of intercession for the weakest and the poorest, who found hope by abandoning themselves to God's will.

The Bishop of Montreal, Mgr. Ignace Bourget, advocated this same spirit of surrender when he recommended to his flock to pray to Saint Joseph. In August 1855, when Alfred was just ten years old and had already lost his father, he may have heard words drawn from the bishop's pastoral letter: "All of you who ask for great graces, address your prayers to the good, great, and powerful Saint Joseph!" And that is what Alfred decided to do. Faithful to his ancestors' example, he put his trust in life. He decided to live his own life fully, as his relatives had done. Following their example, he would battle his way through life using not just his hands, but his wits, and perhaps most of all, his heart. And whenever possible, he would help others in their own struggle.

Canon Catta, by piecing together the testimony of miscellaneous witnesses, and by uncovering some rare photographs of the Brother—most often taken against his will—left us a fine description of Brother André. "He was a very short man, only five feet three inches tall. He was extremely thin, though well pro-portioned, with the exception of his extremities. His hands, in particular, were very big for a man his size. He always bore his head high, which only drew more attention to his high forehead, furrowed with wrin-kles. Heavy folds of skin sagged from the corners of his mouth, inching down toward a strong, deter-mined chin. His lips were thin and even, his nose was slightly flat. He had kind, mischievously wise eyes: the eyes of a child. Jet-black, almost almond-shaped, they twinkled beneath finely etched eyebrows. With age, his face became a web of fine wrinkles. He had always had something of a sallow complexion, but his wizened face now lent him an expression of constant weariness, an expression belied, however, by the liveliness of his features.

"When he started working at the Oratory, in 1904, Brother André was fifty-nine years old, and the pilgrims always knew him with white hair. He combed his thinning hair from left to right on the top of his head, forming a beautiful silver crown."

The Brother's frail features betrayed the poor health he had borne all his life, a sickliness that only got worse with age. In his last years, his doctors forbade him to climb stairs. At the Oratory, this was tantamount to sentencing him to immobility, since stairways were everywhere. His friends, sympathetic to his plight, used to take him in their arms and carry him to his office. "He weighed no more than a feather," they said. The body of a sick man, or the body of an ascetic: both were fitting descriptions of him.

Brother André's unimposing physique was matched by a terrible shyness; perhaps this was why he could never assert himself. His timidity may have been due to his humble beginnings in life. He had been an orphan, an apprentice, an unskilled worker, an exile, and a porter. How could these experiences have fashioned anything even remotely resembling the serene confidence of the mighty? Of course, this natural inclination to timidity fed on an innate, indeed a virtuous, modesty: throughout his life, out of sincere humility, he refused to acknowledge his worth. When people attempted to thank him for a cure or a blessing, he would forever object, "It's God's doing, not mine at all!" All his life, he shied away from any form of acclaim.

However, in his humility, there was not a trace of melancholy. Short and frail as he was, he used to challenge playfully his athletic friends—firemen, policemen—to mock combats. He would mimic the classic stance of a boxer awaiting battle with fists raised. Brother André never lost his sense of humor, even as he was a daily witness, and a most compassionate one, to human misery.

No matter what he endured in his life, Brother André liked to laugh. And he never hesitated to make a joke or attempt a pun if he knew it could cause others to laugh. He said one day, "Happiness comes from God, and sadness, from the devil." One of his brethren observed, "With the poor and the downcast, he was always cheerful. His happiness was contagious. He spent his days listening to complaints, but he kept saying that one shouldn't be sad, that it was good to laugh a little." And when there was no occasion to laugh, it was not beyond him to create one.

One example: for many years, long before people had heard of Saint Joseph's Oratory, the sanctuary of Sainte-Anne-de-Beaupré, near Quebec City, had attracted crowds of pilgrims. As the fame of the Oratory and its keeper grew, there were allegations—apparently unfounded—that the stream of pilgrims was now being diverted from Quebec City to Montreal. One day, then, a local wit asked, "Tell me, Brother André, just how busy is Saint Joseph these days?" Without missing a beat, the Brother shot back, "Is he busy? Don't even ask. Why, he can hardly find time to shave!"

On another occasion, Brother André received a paralyzed pilgrim in his office. The man was totally incapacitated. The sight of such misery brought tears to the Brother's eyes. He spent some time with his helpless visitor. Eventually the pilgrim took his leave; in front of a crowd of stunned onlookers, he strode out of the office, looking like any healthy young man, and evidently completely cured. Brother André then addressed the crowd, asking for the man's name. Someone cried out, "He's called Mr. Laverdure"— Mr. Green, in English. "Well apparently," laughed the Brother, "our man is once again green!"

This simple form of humor celebrates life and defies suffering. It is the wit of those Canadians of old, famous not only for their capacity for work but for their sense of play. Their lives would have been unbearably sorrowful had they not chosen to lighten them with humor. Such was Brother André's legacy from his ancestors. Such was the lesson he learned as a child, a lesson he never forgot. All his life, he carried with him that very simple, very precious spirit of joy.

CHAPTER 8

THE SAINT

IN ROME, ON May 23, 1982, Alfred Bessette, known the world over by his religious name of Brother André, was pronounced "Blessed" by Pope John Paul II. Thus the Vatican confirmed the common belief, held in Quebec and abroad, that Brother André was a saint.

What sort of a saint could this awkward little man be? Benoît Lacroix, a Dominican priest who covered the televised ceremony from Rome, stated,

> One need not profess sublime sentiments or grand revelations of the spiritual life to become a saint. Saints reach holiness through their everyday life. This is a simple, "practical" form of sainthood, as we would call it back home . . . a saintliness so characteristic of those humble people still close to their roots that it most resembles some wild growth of nature.

Brother André's brand of spirituality was molded by his personal history, as was his ensuing sainthood. Father Lacroix refined his initial analysis by stating,

> Brother André is part of us, he shares in our particular form of spirituality. Throughout our history, there are many examples of what can be called the pioneer spirit, the will to lay foundations, the thirst for new beginnings, the need to stay close to one's roots while still breaking new ground. And when we examine the way Brother André proceeded, what we see is a pioneer at work. He is someone who first devises a project, then organizes it, and, almost unwittingly, structures it until it becomes a memorable achievement. Brother André thus was a true pioneer, steeped in a spiritual tradition which is unmistakably that of a country still in its infancy.

This, then, is Brother André's spiritual characteristic: he was a man of the land, and in his land, he sought to incarnate his understanding of the Lord. His religion was not learned in books, but garnered from everyday life. It came to him on his mother's lap and during his conversations with Father Provençal. It swelled within his being during his long days of backbreaking labor. This is why he used to pray with his whole body; this is why he prayed on his knees for nights on end.

Father Lacroix described admirably both the personality and the spirituality of the little Brother who had just been beatified:

With Brother André, we are very far from a saint like Teresa of Avila but very close to Saint Francis of Assisi. Brother André did not express his inner life through words. He revealed it through his daily actions, as did Saint Francis. We are dealing here with a very particular kind of holiness, a holiness that brings to mind a person like Mother Teresa. People such as these signify their mysticism through concrete action. Even the deepest forms of mysticism need not be expressed verbally. A mystic may be so retiring as to live his whole life without ever giving any intimation of his belief. There lies Brother André's strength: he was a great mystic who never even uttered the word "mysticism." . . .

This appraisal of Brother André as a mystic comes as something of a surprise, though no one would dispute the fact that the Brother was a man of exceptional generosity, gifted with a unique power of intercession, and a man constantly given to prayer and mortification. Nor would anybody question his great devotion to Saint Joseph and his immense love for the Suffering Lord. For all this, it may seem excessive to describe him as a mystic. Still . . .

Mystical life is essentially the unfolding of an intimate relationship with God. A mystic strives to dwell in the heart of God, just as he lets God make his home in his heart. Let us try to see how Brother André struggled to embody, in his own life, a particular conception of God's will.

Recall, first, the will of the Lord:

> Yet, to shame the wise, God has chosen
> what the world counts folly, and to shame
> what is strong, God has chosen what the
> world counts weakness. He has chosen
> things without rank or standing in the
> world, mere nothings, to overthrow the
> existing order. So no place is left for any
> human pride in the presence of God. (1 Cor
> 1:27–29)

It could be objected here that Brother André might well have appeared very powerful to the public eye. He was known the world over, he received people by the thousands, and he was consulted by statesmen. Crowds flocked to him wherever he traveled. In fact, he was, at one point in his life, the most famous man in his country. But at the outset, who could have known what the future held in store for the humble laborer, for the modest porter? With that in mind, the reference to Saint Paul's Epistle to the Corinthians is essential: Brother André confounded the wise, who had accorded him no wisdom at all.

What was unique about the Brother's intimate relationship with God, what was singular about his consuming love for Jesus Christ? One word, perhaps, is enough to define this bond: compassion. One word suffices, if we recall that the word "com/passion" is itself dual, signifying "suffering/with." In that sense, Brother André was compassion incarnate, as he was a most faithful companion to that mystery of suffering, the Passion of Christ.

The word "devotion" does not adequately describe Brother André's love for the Nazarene. It surely can be used to define the faith and affection Brother

André felt for Saint Joseph, in whom he found both a model and a counselor. However, the Brother truly identified with Jesus. He particularly identified with those terrible moments that marked the end of Christ's life. Abandoned by his friends, submitted to human justice, Jesus was subjected to terrible suffering, suffering that Brother André wanted to share—in his heart, in his flesh.

The final hours of Jesus' life are at the very heart of the Christian mystery of redemption. As Jesus explained to the disciples on the way to the village of Emmaus, "Was not the Messiah bound to suffer in this way before entering upon his glory?" In other words, the passage from death to life necessarily calls for suffering, and even for the death of the self. For a long time, Christians believed Jesus' death was in itself the redemptive act. We now better understand that Jesus gives us life by destroying death. Without the Resurrection, death has no meaning, and suffering, even less. If the will to be reborn is the distinctive sign of the Christian, then one must accord that death was necessary for life to be recreated. To die for those you love will always appear to be the greatest proof of your love for them. But death conquered by life—Life Resurrected—gives its deepest meaning to Christian faith.

A life dedicated to the service of others, up to the extreme limits of one's capacities: such is the way of Jesus, which so fascinated the young Alfred and later, Brother André. Recall that, in his youth, he wore a hair shirt to partake in Jesus' suffering. Father Provençal had to convince him not to torture himself so, by arguing that life would surely provide many opportunities for suffering in the service of others. Of all the events related in the Gospels concerning Jesus' existence, Brother André seized upon the Passion as his deepest inspiration for prayer. The imitation of Christ became his way of life.

His friends were aware of this. Joseph Pichette said, using the simple word "devotion" to describe Brother André's spirituality, "His main devotion was to the Passion of Our Lord. He taught us never to separate our devotion to the Virgin Mary from our devotion to Saint Joseph and to Our Lord. All his prayers were linked to his devotion to the Passion of Christ." Another friend stated, "The mystery of the Passion was the constant object of Brother André's meditation, and it was also his main topic of conversation." Finally, one of his brethren remarked, "Every evening, he paid me a visit in my room. He used to lean against my desk, always remaining on his feet, and speak about the Passion, reciting by heart entire passages from the Gospels. . . ."

Alfred Bessette, as has been mentioned, left school as a boy. What time could he have spared, later in life, to read books, religious or profane? Most likely, very little. Still, he knew the Gospels by heart, as many witnesses have confirmed. Though he had trouble reading, he was obviously able to cull from books what he considered essential, namely that which pertained to the life of Jesus. And what was essential, he learned by heart. He was sufficiently familiar with the Scriptures to discuss them for hours on end, reserved as he was.

He brought up many facets of Jesus' life: his parables, his teachings, and his encounters with others.

When Brother André spoke of the Passion, though, his whole being was transformed. He used to shut his eyes, take firm hold of a crucifix, and describe every moment of Christ's agony, from the Garden of Gethsemane to the last breath on the cross. He detailed the flagellation to the very last whiplash. And he dwelt on the most moving moments of the Passion, such as Jesus' meeting with his mother, Mary. One witness recalled, "He spoke of the Passion as if he were experiencing it personally." Another remembered, "We never tired of listening to him." To his friend Arthur Ganz, we owe this comment: "Twice, Brother André gave me his account of the Passion, which took him about two hours each time. I should have liked to hear it a third time, but I did not dare ask." Azarias Claude explained, "When Brother André started on that subject, he could go on forever." The last word goes to Joseph Pichette: "One day, a man—whose life left much to be desired—asked to meet him. Brother André spoke to him for more than three hours about the Passion. We were all very attentive, and deeply moved."

Brother André often said, "The love shown to us by Jesus during his Passion reveals the Good Lord's love for us." These simple words suffice to understand the Brother: he was touched by God's love for us. "Our Lord came, and he suffered for us. Nothing forced him to do so, but he accepted those sufferings because of his love for us." Thereby does passion breed compassion, just as suffering is borne of love.

Brother André's devotion to the Way of the Cross seems quite natural, given that he daily meditated the mystery of the Passion. Perhaps in this particular devotion he was indebted, yet again, to Father Provençal, who had adorned his church with engravings depicting the fourteen Stations of the Cross. As a youth, Brother André had been greatly inspired by them. Years later, he got hold of some booklets extolling the merits of the "Devotion to the Holy Wounds." He was also familiar with a book called *The Imitation of Christ,* a volume prescribing rigorous ascetic practices that closely matched his spiritual leanings. From the small library he kept in his cell, he drew his devotion to the Cross and his descriptions of the last moments of the life of Christ, which took on such importance in his own daily life.

In 1959, many years after Brother André's death, further evidence was gathered of the Brother's identification with his Master's Passion. It came in the form of a letter addressed to the Oratory by the sole witness to a strange episode in the Brother's life. Despite the writer's rather elaborate interpretation of the event, this letter is worth quoting.

The incident took place before the land on the mountain was purchased by Notre-Dame College. A young boy, no older than thirteen or fourteen, called on the college porter. Since Brother André knew the boy's parents well, he invited the youth back the next day so that they might follow together the Stations of the Cross on the mountainside. The boy arrived at four o'clock sharp, as he had promised to.

He noticed that the Brother had nailed to the trees, here and there, little crosses pointing to the Stations of the Cross. Perhaps now should we let this witness share with us his recollection, put on paper some sixty years after the fact:

> Brother André prayed for a long while. He moved quickly from one Station of the Cross to the other. The sound of breaking branches and the rustle of dead leaves filled the air. I followed him from a fair distance. He would turn back and ask, "Are you tired?" "No," I answered. And I really was not. But I was very worried about him, because his face had changed totally, as if he were suffering a lot and had been crying. I was afraid he might collapse. What would I do then, with no one there to help me? I was eager that the whole thing should be done with. My own prayer had nothing to do with the Way of the Cross; it more closely resembled a simple plea. I kept begging, "My Lord, please let him get back to the college safe and sound."
>
> I kept thinking to myself, "I shouldn't have come. All this never would have happened!" Thank God, it all ended well. I am convinced the good Brother André suffered the agony of Jesus Crucified. I saw him fall, and I could hear the sound of swirling leaves as he fell, at each Station we passed. Frankly, I was afraid. . . .
>
> What a relief it was when we came back down from the mountain and reached the road. There, we parted company without further ado. He inquired, "Are you tired?" I replied, "No, I'm not tired, but I am happy that you made it to the road!" He told me, before taking his leave, "Don't

ever speak of this." I have never been able
to fathom the meaning of those parting
words. . . .

Should we give full credence to this tale? More to
the point, how can we distinguish the tale from the
teller, the event from the impression it left on its witness? How can we even explain the Brother's invita-
tion to a child? Was he afraid of being alone in such
circumstances? We will never know. To be sure, the
narrator is the only witness to a long-past event. Still,
might not this tale truly represent Brother André's
deeply felt participation in the Passion of the Lord
he loved so deeply? The confidant of a day ended his
letter by quoting his old friend: "The more you suffer
as you follow the Stations of the Cross, the closer you
come to Jesus Crucified."

Passion and compassion. The second word takes
its meaning from the first. Brother André was aware
that compassion meant suffering shared. And he
willingly chose to lead a life of compassion.

By uniting, through his very life, human suffering with that of Christ, he transfigured human suffering itself. Brother André served his fellowmen;
he prayed for them, he welcomed pilgrims, he visited and sometimes healed the sick. By doing so, he
embodied Jesus' compassion for the sick, the poor,
and the weak. He bore the sufferings of others, so as
to reveal to them the existence of another life, of an
otherworldly love.

We have already mentioned that Brother André
was perhaps particularly sensitive to human suffering because of his own miserable youth. He had
either witnessed or personally experienced sickness,

weakness, solitude, neglect, or despair. Having thus known suffering in all shapes and forms, he sincerely strove to unburden the unfortunate souls that came to him for help. But, by the same occasion, he wanted them to sense—almost physically—the strength of God's love for them. So that they, too, might exclaim, as he so often did, "How good the Good Lord is!"

He knew, intuitively yet certainly, that in order to become the instrument of God's love, he had to imitate Him as much as he could. He practiced mortification to a degree deemed "heroic" by the Church, as is canonically required by the beatification procedures. Like Jesus, he took it upon himself to relieve people's sufferings. Such a vocation calls for many virtues; Brother André exercised these with a zeal so remarkable that it could only draw public notice. Innumerable witnesses have left us accounts of his virtues, the first of which was charity, expressed through compassion.

Brother André was no biblical scholar. But he was sufficiently familiar with the Epistles of Saint Paul to recognize that "If I have no love, I am nothing." His friend Azarias Claude stated, "Naturally, Brother André had a good heart . . . but I believe it's out of love for God that he looked after the sick, the poor, and the downtrodden." Brother André himself summarized the meaning of his actions, in a few well-chosen words: "The Lord is our elder brother. We, the little brothers, must thus love one another as members of the same family."

Canon Catta further detailed the Brother's exercise of virtue:

Brother André practiced charity in a silent and retiring manner. He was retiring for fear of being in someone's way. He was always "afraid of disturbing others." He was silent out of discretion. One could be sure that a confidence made to him would never be repeated. He never kept records of his meetings and never revealed the identity of his callers. He had total respect for others, from which followed the respect others showed him.

His was the silence of forgiveness. He never said a word against his enemies, nor did he ever speak in bitterness. He sought to justify people's failings by pointing to their weakness or ignorance. He used to change the course of a conversation should it take on an uncharitable turn. On such occasions, he might attempt to place one of his famous puns, although he knew perfectly well how lame they were. He explained, "My wit may be unsubtle, but at least it is not uncharitable!" To those people who would detract their peers, he would peremptorily exclaim, "Be quiet!" He preferred describing his fellowmen as "good people." And his general rule was, "Try to be cheerful, rather than sad; but be very careful never to hurt anyone's feelings!"

Canon Catta called him "the Good Samaritan of Mount Royal." He could not have found, in the Gospels, a comparison more fitting to the little Brother.

A man truly charitable will always choose to defend the weak. Joseph Pichette left us a personal recollection that illustrates Brother André's particular love for the poor: "When I started seeing Brother André, I was poor. And as I recall, he was more concerned with me in my days of poverty than he was when I started making a little money. . . ." Pichette added, "He received poor people with even more warmth than he accorded to the rich." Brother André made no concessions as he practiced that most unequivocal of virtues, charity.

THE "GOOD BROTHER"

This charity, this special care and respect for his fellowmen—humble as they may be—may well have sprung from Brother André's own upbringing. However, even as he led a life of practical generosity, he sought to respect scrupulously his religious commitment. In this regard, he was indeed a "good Brother."

When he was the college porter, he used to say, "I have to follow the rule. It's very important." He sometimes regretted being unable to meet every obligation of the rule because of the sheer number of requests pilgrims addressed to him. On such occasions, he used to say, "If people only understood! I'd have more time to give to community life." In several instances, he may have felt torn between duty and charity. In itself, his work as a porter isolated him from his colleagues: he slept in his porter's lodge, took his meals apart from the rest of the community, and was invariably busy when his brethren enjoyed their brief moments of leisure. Then, very early on, he started receiving people, first at the college lodge and later in the tramway shelter. Finally, and perhaps foremost, there was the psychological isolation borne of his special mission, which only abated with time. It was not an easy task to live a communal life, to be as one with others, in such unfavorable circumstances. He may well have lived in a community, but he lived alongside, not with, his brethren. He was conscious of this; it embarrassed and pained him.

Brother André detested gossip and felt unable to engage in any kind of conversation with his colleagues. He used to say, in his own defense, "I can't see myself sitting at the same table with the others. . . . I wouldn't know what to say to priests." To those who condemned his silence, he replied, "But, Father, you priests are theologians. I would rather listen to what you say." Despite his explanations, there was a certain malaise within the community: Brother André's exchanges with his brethren were rare, almost nonexistent.

Still, Father Arthurius Théorêt, who lived close to the Brother for sixteen years, stated that he never heard from him a single word of reproach addressed against his community. He deferred to all his brethren, even when he obtained little respect in return.

Little by little, though, his very generosity convinced his fellows of the strength of his religious commitment. Father Deguire recalled how he often would hear Brother André reciting his rosary late into the night. He once suggested to him that he might take better care of his health. "Has it never occurred to you," he said to the Brother, "that your rest could also be a form of prayer?" Brother André stared at him with an "unforgettable expression in his eyes" and said, "Father, if only you saw the state of the people who commend themselves to me, you wouldn't ask me that." He prayed alone, and he prayed endlessly. Joseph Pichette sometimes shared Brother André's room, and he recalled, "Right before going to bed, he'd pray once more, and he'd ask me to pray with him. On some evenings, he was so exhausted that he'd take a fifteen-minute rest, and when he awakened, he continued his prayers. Sometimes, he'd go down to the chapel to pray for most of the night. One time, I was a little worried, and I went downstairs to check on him. He was on his knees praying, with his head profoundly bowed."

Father Théorêt summed up Brother André's religious life in a few words:

> His devotion to prayer, the very way he attended Mass or followed the Stations of the Cross, his rapt attention during the Hour of Adoration of the Blessed Sacrament were as many signs testifying to an intense life of faith. His rare conversations usually concerned obedience to his Superiors, religious poverty, or observance of both silence and the rule.

Thus, Brother André lived his religious life as best he knew.

He also practiced mortification. This he did, on the one hand, by attending the sick, either by receiving them at the Oratory or by visiting them in their homes, and on the other hand, by self-imposed penance. In this regard, his diet may have seemed questionable, given that his purpose was to be useful to others. His friends sometimes felt he was uselessly weakening an already frail body. His usual menu? The least food possible. "He never takes a good meal!" said people around him, probably referring to Brother André's favorite dish, a little flour mixed with hot water. Once, when he was dining with his friend Pichette, he asked for one of his favorite desserts, a blancmange. He gave the following recipe for the delicate jelly-like dish: "Simply boil some wheat and cornstarch in milk neither sweetened nor salted"! On certain rare occasions, he would allow himself a traditional French-Canadian dish, such as pea soup or pork beans. When he had guests over to share a meal, in his room above the chapel, he used to serve them meat, or to be more precise, "a piece of beef simmering in water, to which he added a pinch of flour." That was the menu for feast days!

In short, Brother André ate little, and he ate poorly. Of course, because of his weak digestion, he could not have stomached elaborate dishes had he tried to. In this respect, virtue and sickness are scarcely distinguishable. What is certain is that he chose to live the life of the poor. Fine meals would have gone against the spirit of poverty, which was dearer to him than his own health.

The Brother wore his cassock until it was falling into shreds. He often said, "There's no point in seeking material comfort because it's more difficult, then, to follow God's way, as one should." In this vein, his friend Azarias Claude left us the following anecdote:

I noticed one day that Brother André needed a new overcoat. I made him understand that this really was a necessity, not a luxury. He finally agreed to get a new coat if his Superior consented to it. Permission was easily obtained, although I was the one who did the asking. Brother André wanted to buy a secondhand coat or a very inexpensive one. I brought him to a tailor. He objected to my choice of cloth, saying it was too beautiful and too expensive. I had to tell him I would no longer want to be seen with him in his frayed old coat. He again insisted that I first obtain his Superior's permission for this purchase. And only then did he agree to buy the new coat. He wore it for another fifteen years.

There was no wasting money with this Brother! Another friend recounted, "Brother André and I were in Sherbrooke. In the car, I clumsily sat on his hat. He said to me with a smile, 'I've had this hat for 22 years now, and you had to go and sit on it and ruin it!'" Should we call this good-humored thrift?

Things only got worse when it came to shoes, although the Brother's friend Joseph Pichette was in the "shoe business," to borrow his own term. He recalled, "Brother André showed me his hopelessly worn shoes and asked me, 'Would it cost a lot to mend them?' I had him try on a new pair, and I gave them to him. He was about to leave, and as I was throwing his old shoes away, he asked for them back. 'But they're no good!' I said to him. 'That is not for you to decide,' he replied. And I had to give them back to him."

He was totally indifferent to any form of luxury. For example, he was sometimes chauffeured in a Cadillac, or sometimes in a small car. He did not even notice the difference. "As long as it has four wheels and it moves, it's all the same to me," he used to say. His room was simply furnished, with only the bare necessities. He kept it tidy by himself. He could not abide being attended by the Sisters who usually did the housekeeping. Even in his own community, he frowned on any intimation of extravagance. Of a mere copper staircase railing, he once said, "It looks like gold! This is much too rich for men of the cloth."

Another practice of poverty became an integral part of Brother André's life: he exercised absolute obedience, surrendering his will to that of his Superiors. He followed the community rule to the letter, even if his special ministry allowed him some latitude, as it set him apart—at least physically—from his brethren.

For instance, his evening visits to the sick were planned by his Superiors, who chose both the people visited and the number of visits. Even when he was very tired, he drove himself to make all the required rounds.

It was the same with his trips to the United States. It was not sufficient to have permission to go there; he refused to leave without specific orders from his Superiors. He knew he would see family and friends over there, but he always insisted on having work to do as well. His schedule had to include visits to the sick and the poor. He had quite simply surrendered his will. He was well aware of this, and totally lucid about his decision. He once said, "The Good Lord gives extraordinary strength to an obedient Brother. Sometimes, when He wants a soul to suffer, He may cloud a Superior's judgment. For instance, you may be overworked and still be asked to do more. Accept, even then. You should always obey your Superiors' decisions." Even when excessive demands were made upon him, or when he knew others were at fault, he would still obey. Abandoning one's own will is perhaps the greatest sign of poverty.

AN ALL TOO HUMAN SAINT

Believers tend to think holiness is the achievement of perfection. Therefore, a saint should lead a life in all ways exemplary, a life free from all human imperfections, a life as angelic as it is ascetic. The lives of the saints show just how flawed this conception of sainthood is. Saints are indeed admired for their virtues, but it is their little weaknesses that endear them to us. Brother André was admirably virtuous, yet he knew his limits all too well. Some of his failings were obvious. This did not stop people from respecting him. They simply acknowledged that the man had not yet managed to tame a sometimes impulsive nature. No, Brother André was not perfect.

In the morning, as he prepared to receive hundreds of visitors, he used to say that he was going to his "*bourreau*"—a pun on the French words *bureau* (office), and *bourreau* (torturer). In other words, his office hours were pure torture. The hours spent listening to people's complaints sometimes brought

him close to exasperation. Unfortunately, his temper
sometimes got the better of him. Some virtuous witnesses claimed, "I never saw him being impatient
with anyone. . . . I never once saw him angry or
short-tempered. . . ." Well, those people missed
memorable scenes. Brother André himself admitted
to losing his composure on occasion. One witness
even stated, "I saw Brother André lose his patience
four or five times, every afternoon, when there
were huge crowds of pilgrims." Whom should one
believe? Perhaps the most trustworthy voice belongs
to Brother André's Superior, Father Cousineau. He
knew the Brother from 1909 to the year of his death,
in 1937. Who could have observed him better, who
could give a more balanced account of the Brother's
alleged "moods" than Father Cousineau? This is his
testimony:

> During the early years of his work, Brother
> André rarely showed any signs of impa-
> tience, at least not to my knowledge. As
> he neared the end of his life, especially in
> the last three or four years, he did indeed
> express his impatience more frequently.
>
> Many people, frightened by his ascetic
> expression or by the abruptness with which
> he put an end to meaningless conversa-
> tions, failed to notice that Brother André
> maintained, despite his abrupt demeanor,
> a facial serenity [which was] the mirror
> of his inner peace. . . . His outbursts of
> impatience were attributable, at least in my
> opinion, to his old age, to his failing health,
> and to the weariness his work caused
> him—after all, he was on his feet for hours

on end as he worked. Finally, one must take into consideration the ever-increasing demands made upon him by the throngs of visitors who came to his office. Some displays of impatience served to caution against immodest dress. On occasion, they were meant to lead to a more enlightened form of faith those misguided souls who thought that Brother André was a "miracle man." Finally, I can assure you that Brother André never tried to justify his behavior, in those circumstances, by saying he had been right to act as he had; on the contrary, he suffered terribly from his lapses, suffered to the point of weeping. . . .

The following examples depict those situations in which the good Brother was particularly prone to losing his poise. Once a woman came to him demanding a cure. Brother André told her, with his special brand of humor, "Madam, you've seen quite a few doctors, you've paid them good money, and still you weren't cured. Here, it won't cost you a penny. Does God owe you anything?" To which the woman answered, "Oh yes indeed. I go to Communion every morning." And the Brother countered, "Well, then, if the Good Lord owes you something, go and collect your due yourself. I'm not here to pay for God."

On another occasion, an American visitor asked him to explain how he managed to cure people: was it through magic or hypnotism? Brother André lost his temper. He ordered the man thrown out, and shaking with emotion, said to him, "Get out, you're a scoundrel!"

He was also known to be severe, if not harsh, with certain women. Brother André was a very modest man: apparently, he had trouble tolerating what he considered indecent attire. To a lady who was wearing a sleeveless dress, he gave a medal, recommending that she rub herself with it until her sleeves grew back! To another woman he said more pointedly, "I'm afraid you're at the wrong place. Go and get dressed and then you can come back." To another still, "You say you have a sore throat? Perhaps if you covered it a bit, you'd be healed." Or, "Keep your five dollars to buy clothes to cover your chest." Women who sported low-necked dresses or short skirts wore clothes that were, in his opinion, "too low at the top and too high at the bottom." If the skirt was long enough but the blouse too revealing, he would say, "Cut off a piece of your skirt and add it to your blouse." His most abrupt repartees: "Madam, is that a bathing suit you're wearing?" And: "You seem to have forgotten to put on a dress!"

Brother André's modesty in matters of dress may appear, by contemporary standards, to border on scrupulousness. Both fashions and mentalities have changed a great deal since the 1920s. We should note, however, that he attempted to use humor to lighten embarrassing situations. His reactions were those of a simple man: direct, unbending, and somewhat brusque. Of course, Brother André was no more scrupulous than were other clerics of his time, although his modesty was exceptional. We should not forget that, even as a youth, he chastened his body by wearing a hair shirt. Sensual pleasures were totally foreign to him. On the subject, he was inflexible. Father

Deguire observed, "It was, in a way, an instinct of defense, a way of protecting his morals."

Perhaps we should not be overly surprised by these sudden outbursts of temper. Brother André received millions of visitors; he had to address their grievances and sometimes to bear with their peculiar ways or behavior. He would have had to be a saint not to show more impatience!

Joseph Pichette summed it all up, perhaps with a little friendly indulgence:

> I knew Brother André for 30 years, and I spent whole days with him in his office, even in suffocatingly hot weather, with pilgrims jostling him from morning to night. I noticed that he always had a kind word for all. He was cheerful and in as good a mood at the end of the day as he had been in the morning. This was especially true during the first 25 years I knew him. In the last five years of his life, age caught up with him, he got tired faster, and he was more nervous. . . .

In this respect, Brother André was quite like those worthy people we know and admire, people we might find remote were it not for their human frailty.

CHAPTER 9

FROM CHAPEL
TO CHURCH

ON AUGUST 2, 1908, a journalist from a local
paper covered the inauguration of the new chapel
on the mountain. Carried away by prophetic inspiration, he wrote: "Clearly, this sanctuary is fated to
become a great place of pilgrimage."

To which omens did the writer owe his flight of
fortuitous prophecy? The correspondent may have
been impressed by the astonishing number of believers straining to hear the Mass: they were seven hundred on that inaugural day, huddled around a chapel
that could seat only fifty. Perhaps the reporter had
heard that in the preceding four years, there had been
countless individual or group visits to the very first
chapel. Most likely, our journalistic soothsayer was
only stating the obvious: Brother André's fame was
growing steadily. Increasing numbers of sick people
sought his help and found at his side either the
strength to bear their affliction or an actual cure. A

few months earlier, in March 1908, a medical certificate had confirmed, for the first time, a recovery inexplicable from a scientific point of view. Father Dion,
who was very prudent and circumspect in these
matters, declared in his Sunday sermon, "It has been
stated unequivocally that Brother André, the porter
at Notre-Dame College, performed a miracle."

Brother André might well receive visitors by the
thousands; he still had no say as to where he could
greet them. That is, until 1908, when a group of sixteen
fervent friends of the Brother took upon themselves
to promote and eventually to build a larger chapel.
They formed a committee: M. Maucotel acted as
president, J. A. Renaud as secretary, and T. A. Durand
as treasurer. Not only did they ask for a chapel
large enough to accommodate the increasing crowds
attending prayer services, but they also solicited "the
permission to build a lodging accommodating two
persons, to be the custodians of the Oratory and its
sacred objects." To convince the college authorities,
they circulated a petition that was soon signed by
two thousand people. They asked for no money from
the Holy Cross Congregation. The $5,000 needed to
build the new chapel would come from private donations. From the very beginning, people who had been
healed wanted to show their gratitude to Brother
André. As soon as the new chapel opened its doors,
an impressive collection of crutches, canes, and other
orthopedic devices was displayed to mark the exceptional nature of the sanctuary.

Brother André had been involved personally in
only the first steps of the building of the chapel. He
had cleared paths leading to the future chapel before

actual construction had commenced. As for the erection of its wooden frame, he had left that work to people competent in the building trade. He was already kept busy enough with his various duties. Until 1910, he was only the college porter, and all his "spare time" was spent receiving the sick.

He also did not want material concerns to interfere with the more spiritual nature of his work. For example, when his friends set up a small counter in the chapel to sell objects of piety, he found it distasteful that a sacred place should house commercial activity. Accordingly, his friends decided to build a separate edifice, better suited to commerce. The new building was composed of a souvenir shop; a room for Brother André, by now the keeper of the Oratory; and a waiting room for pilgrims who came to consult him. Thus the Oratory became better equipped to meet the needs of individual travelers or groups of pilgrims.

Soon a beautiful new bell, brought over the Atlantic from France, would call the faithful to Mass. The blessing ceremony of the bell was scheduled for June 6, 1909. The original committee of supporters seized the occasion to promote the devotion to Saint Joseph, the patron saint of the Oratory. They distributed throughout Montreal a leaflet describing the activities taking place at the Oratory. The heading of the leaflet bore these words: "Saint Joseph's Oratory of Mount Royal." Thus, for the first time, reference was made to the now familiar name of the sanctuary. The preliminary passages inviting people to pray to Saint Joseph carried this brief explanation: "A little sanctuary has been built in his honor, amid trees and flowers, on the flank of Mount Royal facing Notre-Dame College. Already, this humble sanctuary has witnessed truly remarkable recoveries and conversions. Every day, many pious souls come to pray here, either alone or in groups." The call to the faithful was heard. A crowd of three thousand people gathered for the blessing of the new bell, a portent of the endless crowds of pilgrims who would visit the Oratory for years to come.

To make it easier for the faithful to reach the chapel, wooden walkways were built, which wound their way up the mountain from the street below. The Oratory was equally being readied for the countless visitors who would attend, in Montreal, the Eucharistic Congress of 1910. Brother André quickly became aware that he could not do everything by himself. He argued, "Without the assistance of a priest, my mission cannot be fully achieved." And to emphasize his dilemma, he painted this sorry tableau: "I need the assistance of a priest. Pilgrims come here, and they have to ask to be blessed by an old thing like me!"

His Superior heeded Brother André's request. He appointed Father Adolphe Clément, a brilliant and promising young priest, unfortunately hampered by failing eyesight, to assume the responsibilities that the keeper of the Oratory could not fulfill. As has been mentioned previously, upon taking on his new duties, Father Clément recovered his eyesight, to the utter amazement of his oculists. He became "Brother André's right-hand man, his gift from Providence." The relationship between the two associates is described here in an unusual manner, given that in the religious hierarchy of the day, Brothers were ordinarily at the service of priests. . . . Father Clément's presence proved to be indispensable: during the Eucharistic Congress, some two hundred thousand pilgrims—bishops, priests, and simple believers alike—went to the mountain to pray at the Oratory.

One of the attendants of the Eucharistic Congress, Father Alexis Lépicier, who later became a cardinal, could hardly contain his enthusiasm: "We are witnessing here the rapid rise of a sanctuary dedicated to the holy Patriarch, where heavenly graces and favors are profusely dispensed. This sanctuary will become the Lourdes of Canada." The comparison may appear excessive. At the time, the Oratory consisted only of a simple wooden chapel. Some might say that the future proved Father Lépicier right!

The crowds were already considerable. As early as 1910, three daily Masses were celebrated. The correspondence received at the Oratory was also immense: from November 21, 1909, to October 28, 1910, no less than 24,745 letters were sent there by pilgrims. Out of that number, 112 mentioned "complete recoveries"; 4,329, marked improvement; and 313, special favors obtained, including several conversions.

The Archbishop of Montreal, Mgr. Bruchési, set up a commission of inquiry to study the extraordinary events unfolding at the Oratory, events attributed to Saint Joseph by way of Brother André's intercession. The Provincial Superior, Father Dion, declared at a hearing that "Brother André does appear to be Saint Joseph's favored instrument." He also expressed his total confidence in the "Brother whose humility and simplicity are exemplary." The commission heard several witnesses, who spoke of their recoveries in front of physicians and theologians. The commission's conclusions were cautious. But its investigators stated that "the extraordinary facts we were able to study also appear to point to a supernatural intervention, due to the benevolence and power of Saint Joseph."

Two years later, on November 17, 1912, Mgr. Bruchési presided over a ceremony in the small chapel. He expressed in unambiguous terms his faith in the Oratory, using words that must have heartened Brother André. For the archbishop assured the little Brother that he had the entire confidence of the official authorities of his diocesan church. Mgr. Bruchési predicted the expansion of the Oratory. His own speculation went far beyond Brother André's modest dream:

> At this Oratory, Saint Joseph shall be honored in a special way, as is the Holy Virgin at Lourdes and Loreto. I see here the unfolding of a movement of piety that soothes my soul greatly. In the very beginning, a pious man put up a statue in this place. Every day, people came here to pray. Before long, a small chapel was built. But as those good people devoted to Saint Joseph arrived here in ever-larger numbers, it was necessary to enlarge it on more than one occasion. Work has just begun here, and I can foresee, in a not too distant future, the construction on Mount Royal of a basilica worthy of Saint Joseph, merging on this most splendid of horizons.

Might I say miracles are happening
here? If I were to deny it, all these instruments, silent witnesses to so much suffering, would speak in my place. I need no
inquiry [to convince me]. . . . There are,
most certainly, extraordinary events taking
place here . . . and greater wonders than the
healing of the body. . . .

A GREAT CHURCH

Did Brother André even desire greater honors for
Saint Joseph? Had he ever imagined that the small
chapel might one day become a great basilica?

Nothing is less certain. Quite simply, it was not in
character with the humble Brother to entertain such
grandiose dreams. He liked simple things, and he
disapproved of any intimation of luxury, especially
in a house of worship. In his mind, the chapel, as
it existed, may have satisfied his initial objective,
which was to have a place in which to pay homage
to Saint Joseph. It seemed natural that Brother André
should be the keeper of the chapel, but only as long
as it remained what it was meant to be: a simple
place, where one greeted simple folk, and where one
prayed to the very model of simplicity.

And yet the crowds grew bigger, the pilgrimages
more frequent, the needs of the faithful more pressing. Brother André may not have cherished the dream
of building an awesome basilica. But it is evident that
nothing was dearer to his bishop's heart. In a letter to
Father Dion, dated from January 1914, Mgr. Bruchési
wrote: "I wholeheartedly authorize you to build a

159

church on Mount Royal in honor of Saint Joseph. This church will replace the temporary chapel."

Clearly, in the eyes of Mgr. Bruchési, the small chapel could only be "temporary." And Father Dion was in full agreement. Brother André himself may have come, with time, to believe in the necessity of an imposing house of worship dedicated to Saint Joseph. We know that he went with Father Dion to meet with the archbishop when time came to get the latter's approval for the enlargement of the first little chapel. He must have supported the project put forward by his Superiors and friends. For the larger the church, the more it would attract pilgrims, and the more Saint Joseph would be glorified.

But the Superior General of the Order of the Holy Cross was much more hesitant. He voiced several reservations, most of them concerning the twin fates of the Oratory and its original founder. After Brother André's death—he was then close to seventy years old—would pilgrims continue to come to the mountain to pray to Saint Joseph? To be sure, the devotion to Jesus' foster father was rapidly gaining ground in Montreal; but was it not a fact that many pilgrims came to the Oratory simply to beg for Brother André's intercession? Was it not equally true that many came looking only for a cure? Was not the Brother's reputation as a miracle-worker the real attraction at the sanctuary? What would happen when he was no longer there?

In a letter sent by the Superior General of the Order, Father Gilbert Français, to Brother Marie-Auguste, who was then acting as secretary to Brother André, the first wrote:

There seems to be among our Canadian brethren such pressure to build and to hastily assemble a grand design that, even from here, I am slightly frightened by the whole matter. The church that people are dreaming of building above the Oratory will cost a fortune. Because, of course, it must be immense and splendid, and because of the simple expense of hoisting construction materials onto the mountain. There is too much uncertainty, risk, and possible error linked to this vast enterprise.

Another letter sent to Brother Marie-Auguste by an assistant of Father Français inquired,

I would like to know exactly how much money has been put aside by the Oratory for the construction project. Let me convey to you the opinion of the Very Reverend Father General on the subject. He believes that all very much depends on Brother André, and he fears that when the Brother is gone, the number of pilgrims may decrease. . . . We must proceed with utmost caution, so as not to face a financial fiasco similar to the one of the Lourdes parish church. Are you absolutely positive that donations will follow, once actual construction begins?

According to the architectural drafts, construction costs were valued at $100,000, a large sum for the time. But the amount was already lying in the coffers of the Order. It was felt it would not be too rash to begin work on the venture.

At least the first stage could be commenced without undue trepidation, although the scope of the project as a whole was admittedly ambitious, if not presumptuous. The architects' plans for the future Oratory were divided into different stages. The first one comprised only the construction of a crypt; it would serve eventually as a sort of substructure for a great basilica, in the Italian style, crowned by a dome overlooking the city. The early plans of the architectural firm of Viau and Venne are very similar, in their main features, to what the Oratory looks like today. It took amazing daring simply to consider the undertaking of such a complex project. After all, only ten years had elapsed since the building of the small chapel. To replace the humblest of churches, plans were being laid out for what would be the biggest, the most grandiose and awesome of basilicas.

On July 11, 1914, Father Dion, the Provincial Superior of the Holy Cross Order, received a letter from his Superior General: "You are granted all necessary permission to begin immediately the construction of Saint Joseph's church. . . ." Five days later, Father Dion obtained the official approval of Mgr. Bruchési, who expressed his renewed confidence in the project: "I endorse with great joy your project as submitted, in all conformity with the permission granted you by the general chapter of your Order. . . . You may count on the generosity of Saint Joseph's many servants."

All the parties concerned now had given their approval: the diocesan authorities, the Holy Cross Order, the committee of supporters, and Brother André himself. Whether the latter's consent weighed much on the unfolding of events is a matter open to debate. One can only imagine that the Brother was interested in the project, just as one can readily surmise that he had no executive power. His role was in no way a material one. He remained content to apply himself to what he knew best, that is, prayer.

A construction committee was formed, consisting of the Provincial Father, the Superior of Saint-Laurent College, the bursar of Notre-Dame College, and the "Very Honorable Brother André." Although he had no desire to be involved personally in the construction of the basilica, the Brother carried his share of responsibility in the enterprise. Along with his Superiors and his friends, he committed himself fully to this great adventure of faith, the scope of which went far beyond his humble aspirations.

A NEW ADVENTURE

Even today, one struggles to envision the magnitude of the project. At the time, it certainly seemed to outweigh—by far—the means of its promoters.

The architectural firm commissioned for the work submitted a design that was tantamount to tackling the mountain itself. Tons of rock had to be moved to lay the foundations for the future church, at two different land levels. The first stage itself, the construction of a crypt, seemed fraught with difficulties. Even the crypt surely would cost more than the $100,000 collected. Indirect costs were predictable, since whole parts of the mountain had to be blown up with dynamite, in order to nestle the future church.

Furthermore, the interior of the temple could not be left bare. Inside the crypt, there would be a marble statue, beautiful stained-glass windows, and benches for some fifteen hundred people—expenses not initially accounted for in the first architectural plans.

The administrators of the affairs of the Oratory may be forgiven for being wary of the second stage of construction. For the crypt had been defined as a foundation: logically, then, it called for the construction of an edifice far more impressive, a second church built in the following years. After all, one does no great honor to a saint by dedicating to him a mere substructure! All concerned actors, including Brother André, envisioned a grand design for the Oratory, which would not be complete without a basilica.

The second stage thus seemed fated to be even more challenging than the first. The ground on the higher slopes of the mountain lay on solid rock. Exceptional engineering skills would be required to dig, displace, and level the land so that it could support a high, heavy structure. But for the time being, the work at hand was the construction of the crypt. What admirable faith these builders showed! Literally, they had the faith that moves mountains.

In August 1914, Germany declared war on France. Great Britain joined the war, thereby engaging its dominions in the hostilities. There was of course no fighting on Canadian soil, but young men left for England to serve under the British flag, leaving behind their worried families.

In the winter of 1915, there was an increase in the number of pilgrims at the Oratory. Father Dion, a contributor to the *Saint Joseph Annals*, published by the Oratory from 1911 on, wrote: "Since the beginning of this year, marked by the terrible anguish brought on by the war, trust in the blessed patriarch Saint Joseph has grown proportionately to the number of people in mourning or need." Huge crowds of pilgrims gathered for Saint Joseph's feast day on March 19; according to Father Dion, "Tramway conductors claimed that 10 to 15 thousand people got off at the Notre-Dame College stop."

On May 11, 1916, out of five bidding contractors, the construction committee selected the Boileau Construction Firm to take charge of work. The company submitted an estimate of $175,000, with an additional $30,000 going toward interior decoration. This represented a fair increase with regard to the initial costs submitted to the Order's Superior General. But the latter, who at first had been so reluctant, simply wrote to Father Dion: "You can go ahead. I am as convinced as you are that with two years in construction costs already covered, you will successfully complete your project, and that the necessary resources will be forthcoming."

Construction started on May 19. During the summer, crowds of pilgrims on their way to Mass mingled with construction crews. Father Dion wrote in the *Annals:*

> The outlying areas of the Oratory look like the trenches furrowing the plains of France and Flanders. Explosives pulverize great slabs of rock, as the land is cleared to make way for the immense crypt. It sounds like thunder and machine-gun fire. . . .

Fortunately, there have been no accidents
so far, even with all the pilgrims rushing
up and down the dusty, rock-strewn hillside paths.

By the summer of 1917, the exterior walls of the
crypt were completed, and the finishing touches
were being applied to the interior of the building.
Everything seemed to be falling into place, and
everyone looked forward to an imminent inauguration. But there was one last problem to be dealt with.
A vital part of the interior decoration was still missing. Fortunately, Brother André's secretary put the
whole story down on paper. His style, both guileless
and confident, reflects the spirit of his peers, a spirit
of simple faith that sustained the entire venture. In
this regard, the secretary's narrative is worth quoting
in full:

> The final touches were being brought to the
> interior of the sanctuary in the last months
> of 1917. The installation of the choir wood-
> work went smoothly; the superb main
> altar, all of white marble, was slowly tak-
> ing shape; but the statue of Saint Joseph
> was still missing. We were informed that
> the huge crate had left Italy and was cross-
> ing the ocean on a ship heading toward
> New York City. These were the days when
> enemy submarines made many victims,
> as they mercilessly torpedoed passenger
> ships and cargoes; even a hospital-ship
> had been sunk. Would the ship carrying
> the statue escape the Germans' furor? We
> worried constantly. But Saint Joseph was
> protecting his ship, as well as the people

crossing the seas with him. A telegram from New York brought us great joy. The case containing the statue had arrived safely and was now ready to be brought to Canada. However, our trials were not over. The huge package, now at the Montreal customs, could not be picked up because the necessary transfer papers were missing. At last, after a mighty battle with red tape, permission to retrieve it was obtained on November 28th, a Wednesday, the very day of devotion to Saint Joseph. And the next Wednesday, December 5th, the huge crate, which weighed 5,500 pounds, made its way up the mountain, drawn by four horses. On Thursday the 6th, around four o'clock, the statue was heaved onto its pedestal, in the presence of Messrs. Venne, the architect, and U. Boileau, the contractor. Also present were the Reverend Father Rector and humble Brother André, the promoter of the devotion to Saint Joseph at the Oratory, who, at last, was witnessing the glorification of his favorite saint. . . .

On December 17, the newspaper *Le Canada* read, "There was an imposing ceremony yesterday morning at Saint Joseph's Oratory. His Excellency Mgr. Bruchési solemnly blessed the new crypt dedicated to Saint Joseph, amid a large concourse of people. . . ."

The next year, a terrible epidemic, the "Spanish flu," hit Montreal. This deadly form of influenza killed 3,409 persons within two short months. Before long, twenty-four thousand people were sick with the disease. Among the victims were many people dear to Brother André, not least of them his secretary for the past eight years, Brother Marie-Auguste, and Father Dion, the Brother's most resolute advocate.

The *Religious Week,* the official periodical of the diocese of Montreal, eulogized the priest in this fashion:

> In 1912, he was appointed director of Saint Joseph's Oratory, an important and, in a way, a fragile institution. Need one remind our readers that at this sanctuary events extraordinary—to say the least—have occurred over the last 15 years? We would not presume, in a few lines, to qualify these events. Only the Church has sufficient authority to adjudicate in matters of such import. But it is a fact beyond dispute that every year thousands upon thousands of pilgrims come to the Oratory, from all over the world, to pray to Saint Joseph and to commend themselves to his servant, the humble Brother André; these believers leave comforted and edified, if not always healed of their physical afflictions. . . . Father Dion was, we believe, a man chosen by God to take on this difficult ministry. . . .

Brother André was at the time seventy-three years old. He had reached his goal in life, in a most extraordinary fashion: Saint Joseph now had a church where he could welcome all those who trusted in him. The Brother had just lost valuable allies. But he was still surrounded by friends, zealous supporters, and men of faith. Moreover, thousands of people still beckoned for his help. How could he rest, how could he abandon his flock?

During the years of construction, Brother André had followed the work in progress with great interest. Every morning, before Mass, he went to look at the work site. At noon, rather than taking his meal with the community, he used to grab a piece of bread or some biscuits and watch the workers milling around. He never gave any orders. He did not have to: he was an inspiration to all. Claim as he did that it was all "the Good Lord's doing," and that he was only "Saint Joseph's little dog," everyone knew that without him the Oratory never would have existed. He was the soul of the place. The Oratory was his gift to Saint Joseph.

THE INFLUENCE OF THE ORATORY

The following years at the Oratory were filled with extraordinary events; Brother André was overwhelmed by expressions of gratitude. All kinds of stories circulated about him. As has been mentioned previously, Colonel George H. Ham wrote the Brother's first biography, titled *The Miracle Man of Montreal*. The author, who presented himself not as a Catholic, but simply as a believer, was convinced beyond all doubt by what he saw:

> There are miracles wrought today as there have been through time. . . . As it was in days of old, so it is today. There was a time, especially in recent years, when many non-Catholics sincerely believed that these

> alleged miracles existed only in the igno-
> rant minds of the superstitious followers of
> the Roman Catholic Church. . . . But today,
> thousands upon thousands of educated
> people of all nationalities and creeds are
> convinced that the healer wields a super-
> natural, an almost divine power, exercised
> for the wellbeing of all those who suffer.

Of course, the millions of pilgrims who frequent-
ed the Oratory had never needed such printed arguments. And while Brother André could not possibly
see every last one of them, he still received several
hundred people a day. This was bound to exhaust
the Brother, who was now in his seventies. Yet he still
went to visit the sick at home, driven across the city
by his friends. He never stopped working.

On occasion, he traveled abroad. He went to
Ontario regularly, and even more often to the United
States, to visit his family and those American pil-
grims who were particularly good friends of the
Oratory. For a man of the cloth, in this the dawn of
the century, Brother André was a relentless traveler.

During his beatification procedures, his traveling habits were questioned. Could the Brother meet
his religious obligations if he left his community so
often—sometimes for weeks on end? The issue was
addressed by his witnesses: "He never left without
proper permission from his Superiors, and he never
traveled merely for pleasure. His unique objective
was to visit the sick and the poor and to promote the
devotion to Saint Joseph." In other words, Brother
André gladly visited family members and friends
who were dear to him, but he never would have gone

on a trip that was not primarily pastoral. Michel-Albert Trudel, a friend who had chauffeured him on his long trips, said,

> Before leaving on a trip, I always filled up the gas tank because Brother André didn't want to make any stops, even for meals. A few biscuits and a thermos of coffee were enough for him. We used to speed along winding roads while the Brother recited his rosary. Police officers knew him by sight, and since they knew he must have a good reason to be in such a hurry, they simply would let him fly by.

One of his American biographers, Alden Hatch, wrote: "Brother André obtained as many favors from Saint Joseph for the inhabitants of Rhode Island as he did for those of Montreal." Hatch cited a few examples, such as the testimony given by Lionel Maynard before the ecclesiastical court that sat in Providence, during the beatification procedures:

> Brother André cured me. I was stricken with the rot [tuberculosis] of the spinal vertebrae. This was in 1926. My brother-in-law, Dr. Fulgence Archambault, diagnosed the sickness and referred me to Dr. Maria Danford, a specialist from Providence. I spent four weeks in a hospital, with no change in my condition. I left on crutches. I also had to wear a plaster corset reinforced by an iron brace. On November 29th, I was in excruciating pain. Mr. Philippe Brouillard persuaded me to see Brother André, who was staying with Mr. Boulet.

As he entered the room where the sick were waiting for him, Brother André came straight to me. He asked me what was wrong and told me to get up. I managed a few steps, leaning heavily on my crutches. Then Brother André told me to give him the crutches and made me walk without them, faster and faster. Which I did, without ever feeling any pain, in front of about a hundred people, all moved to tears. That same evening, less than an hour later, I was back with my family, reciting my rosary on my knees. I gave my crutches and surgical corsets to Brother André, who took them back to the Oratory. I believe they are still there today.

This explains the comment made by Mr. Trudel, the Brother's chauffeur, who said, "Sometimes we came back from those trips with a carload of crutches!"

About twice a year, Brother André visited New England, especially the states of Rhode Island, Maine, Massachusetts, Vermont, and New Hampshire. He had worked and lived in some of these parts and, most likely, visited them now, remembering people he had once known there. He felt at home in this region, where so many Canadians had gone to make a living in the factories. Many had then settled there, built churches, and remained faithful to both their mother tongue and their Catholic faith. Certain towns, such as West Warwick, Moosup, Holyoke, Woonsocket, Fall River, and Providence, had large French-speaking populations. Members of the Bessette family had moved to these parts permanently. In New England, where his own kin dwelt, where his own language and faith flourished, Brother André found a home away from home.

The Brother sometimes traveled along the other side of the Hudson River, stopping at Plattsburg, Keeseville, Schenectady, Troy, or Albany. He went to New York City, and of course visited Jersey City, the starting point of the first American pilgrimage to the Oratory, in 1912.

On the road, Brother André usually stayed in presbyteries or in friends' homes. Parish priests prepared their flock for the arrival of the celebrated traveler, who was revered as a saint and trusted as a friend. The Brother listened to the faithful, prayed with them, gave them medals or some of Saint Joseph's oil; when he returned to Montreal, his suitcase was brimming over with donations for the work on the Oratory! These trips were meant to offer him periods of relaxation and rest. Unfortunately, zealous parish priests had such busy schedules planned for him that little time was left for leisure. It is fair to say that he probably never knew a moment's rest in his life.

When not abroad, Brother André could always be found at the Oratory, where each day, each year, more and more pilgrims congregated. In October 1920, the Canadian Association of Catholic Youth organized an immense gathering at the hillside crypt, to celebrate the fiftieth anniversary of the selection of Saint Joseph as the patron saint of Canada. The estimation of the crowds' size varied from source to source. The Montreal newspaper *Le Devoir* counted fifty thousand people, while the diocesan periodical the *Religious Week* spotted one hundred thousand pious souls! The reporter from the latter journal may have been carried away by his own enthusiasm. Nonetheless, his account of the event offers a good description of the large religious gatherings that marked the early part of the century:

> Yesterday, we witnessed an immense religious rally at Saint Joseph's Oratory. It was a breath-taking sight! Our readers, of course, will be familiar with Saint Joseph's Oratory, thanks to our extensive coverage of its history. Indeed, who has not heard of the Oratory and its humble and very extraordinary apostle, Brother André? People from all parts of the land visit the Oratory or write to Brother André. All parts of the land: we of course refer to all parts of the American Continent and even to Europe! In the past sixteen years alone, the devotion to Saint Joseph has grown enormously in those lands, in a way unequaled anywhere else, we believe. A small detail offers proof of the fame of both the Oratory and Brother André: letters mailed from far-away Pennsylvania and addressed simply to "Brother Andrew"—with no additional information—always reach their proper destination. . . .

It is undeniable that, in the 1920s, there was a lot of talk about Brother André. The archives of the Oratory contain an important collection of newspaper articles that give a fair idea of the Brother's popularity. They were garnered from the furthest confines of the American Continent. A few excerpts will allow us to weigh the extent of the little Brother's fame.

The Montreal Star. "A Marvelous Cure Wrought by Brother André. Another case of remarkable healing worked by Brother André has just been reported to us. Four-year-old Moses Vourgeois, the son of Mr. and Mrs. Claude Vourgeois, of Ticonderoga, has recovered the use of his right eye, following a visit by the famous Brother André, during a trip the latter made last fall to Morrisonville, N.Y."

The Catholic Mirror (Springfield, Mass.). "Faithful pilgrims credit Brother André with hundreds of miracles. . . . People graced with blessings due to Brother André's prayers, and pilgrims who have been going to the Oratory for years, now call him the 'Miracle Man.'. . ."

Columbia (Washington, D.C.). "The Miracle Man of Mount Royal. Brother André is the last man in the world who would willingly accept to be called a 'miracle man.' But it remains a fitting description of this holy man, totally dedicated to the supernatural."

Correio de Manhao (Brazil). [The reader will notice a few factual errors, probably due to distance and to the barriers of language, errors that nonetheless bear witness to the original writer's good intentions.] "The Miracles of a Canadian Priest. The fame of Father André, pastor of a Canadian parish named Côte-des-Neiges (Montreal), has reached the United States and drawn reviews in all Yankee newspapers and magazines."

The Los Angeles Examiner. [Brother André was the guest of a rich man from Montreal then residing in Pasadena. The trip was supposed to remain a secret, to allow Brother André some rest. But it was not to be.] "A Famous Healer in Pasadena. There are reports to the effect that the Reverend Brother André, from Montreal, is presently in this city. He is said to have healed the blind, the deaf, and the crippled. His presence among us has been kept a secret so far, except from those needing his help. Brother André twice went to a church where he met with some 500 persons, to whom he brought great comfort. Yesterday, he healed a blind man and a deaf man. One woman, who had limped for years, recovered the full use of her legs and went back home without using her crutches. Today, there were four more cures. Brother André heals only through his prayer."

Pasadena Star-News. "Many Cured by a Famous Priest. Despite efforts to keep his presence in Pasadena a total secret, it was reported to us just yesterday that Brother André of Montreal, who is said to be one of the greatest miracle-workers of the Catholic Church, is on a discreet mission here. It is reported that he has been in Pasadena for the last three days and that he is performing miracles. He has cured the sick and healed cripples—who simply let go of their crutches—all this despite the extraordinary measures his hosts took to ensure the secrecy of his visit."

El Universal de Mexico. "Montreal has its own French-Canadian 'saint,' who has worked 10,000 miracles in the last ten years. Brother André, as the 'saint' is known in Montreal, is a man almost eighty years old, but still alert despite his advanced years. He has a very benign face, black, piercing eyes, and a constant kind smile that makes him very engaging. He lives in a small, modestly furnished room, which is heated by a huge stove. The waiting room was filled with about one hundred people, some suffering physically, and others from the soul. There were people of many nationalities, speaking various foreign languages. Brother André received every one of them with great kindness, and after listening to them, asked a few questions and told them, either in English or in French, 'Personally, I can't do anything at all for you. Only Saint Joseph can do that. Pray to him, confess your sins and he'll help you. . . .' The conversations with each were as brief as they were kind, and the sick left invigorated, feeling lighter in both body and soul. . . ."

This is how people spoke of Brother André, and perhaps this is one of the reasons he attracted more and more visitors. So many were they that, some short time after the inauguration of the crypt, there was talk of furthering the work on the Oratory. The crypt was only a substructure. The true church of Saint Joseph would be the basilica.

CHAPTER 10

SAINT JOSEPH'S
BASILICA

THE INAUGURATION OF the crypt aroused
renewed interest in the Oratory, and over a short period, the number of pilgrims there doubled. Moreover,
as Brother André's fame spread abroad, many people
became intrigued, if not fascinated, by his work.
Of course, the sick still desperately sought out
the "Montreal miracle-worker." But now came the
crowds of onlookers eager to see with their own eyes
all those marvels attributed sometimes to the Brother,
sometimes to his prayers, sometimes to the Oratory.
    In 1920, very few Montrealers owned cars. City
folk traveled to the Oratory on foot, by tramway, or
sometimes even on horse-drawn carriages. Over time,
though, more and more smart cars were spotted near
the sanctuary, and parking space had to be provided
for the "rich." Yes, even the mighty traveled to the
Oratory. In this, of course, they were not alone. In
1920 alone, more than four hundred thousand

visitors, pilgrims and tourists alike, climbed the steps leading to the mountainside church.

The congregation's Superiors were not only wise men, but also wise administrators: they had decided that the construction of the crypt would be financed only by the money already in the coffers of the Order. It would be ruinous to begin borrowing from banks. But wisdom has it limits: when the crypt was inaugurated, its executives had already incurred a considerable debt. Of course, it would have to be acquitted before embarking on another architectural venture, which only promised to be more expensive than had been the first. One can hardly blame these administrators for having second thoughts about the project's completion. The architects' plans seemed threatening, even on paper. They called for construction on a gigantic scale, and financial investments no less staggering.

Strangely enough, the administrator of the diocese, Mgr. Georges Gauthier, seemed to be pressing more than anyone else was for the completion of the venture. So much so that, in 1920, he personally donated $1,000 to the Oratory to help pay the debt contracted in the building of the crypt. The money was accepted with gratitude, but it was not sufficient to convince the more cautious executives of the Oratory.

The Superior, Father Alfred Roy, decided to consult the archbishop on the matter. Recall that Mgr. Bruchési already had shown marked affection for Brother André and great interest in his mission. It was not very likely that he would oppose the project in any way. By appealing to him, the Superior was simply taking every possible measure of precaution. Thus, in February of 1921, Father Roy addressed these words to his bishop:

> Seven years ago, you already agreed that a basilica should be built over the crypt. Of course, we all share the same dream. The crypt, built in 1917, can no longer meet adequately the needs and expectations of pilgrims. Not only is it too small to accommodate the large crowds that gather there, but also it seems too modest, even to the pilgrims' eyes. The faithful from our lands, and even believers from abroad, now bid us to finish what we have begun. Many good men, true Christians all of them, cannot hide their disappointment as they weigh our hesitation and inaction.

It would seem that the Superior would have liked nothing better than to tackle boldly this new venture but was wary of its breadth. He did not want to take such an important decision on his own. If his bishop encouraged him to proceed, he would not have to bear in his conscience the sole responsibility of an almost reckless venture.

The bishop's answer was quite predictable:

> God is clearly with us. Only He is able to achieve such great endeavors with such limited means. We must acquit our debt of gratitude toward our celebrated 'miracle-worker,' just as our love for Him must be expressed by more than words. Consequently, it is with great joy that I give you the permission you seek. I am

hereby confirming to you, in writing, what
I have already said to you many times: to
complete this church, which, I hope, will
become a basilica, I grant you every liberty
to act as seems appropriate.

These unequivocal words of support must have
overcome the Superior's vacillation. The authorities
of the Oratory were virtually bound to proceed with
the construction of the basilica.

We know nothing of the role Brother André
played in this enterprise. Nor do we have any indica-
tion as to what he even thought about it. Naturally,
he had understood the original plans. He knew that
the crypt had been intended as a temporary house
of worship, and he fully realized that the Oratory
of Saint Joseph would not be complete without a
basilica.

Even though he never explicitly voiced his opinion on the matter, Brother André must have been
elated by the turn of events. The greater the homage
paid to Saint Joseph, the more the saint he so revered
would rejoice; surely Saint Joseph also would show
his gratitude by bestowing even more graces on
pilgrims. Such was Brother André's reasoning: take
a step toward Saint Joseph, and he will take one
toward you.

We know that the "founding Brother" sat on the
construction committee. During his various trips, he
also accepted all kinds of contributions for the real-
ization of the Oratory. He never expressly asked for
anything, but he received many donations, whether
in Montreal or on his trips abroad. Of course, he
remained devoted almost exclusively to prayer and

to the needs of the Oratory pilgrims. He knew his ministry would be rewarded eventually by thankful prayer or goodwill.

Thus his most active participation in construction was achieved through prayer. After all, the Oratory was meant to be the expression of popular piety, the manifestation of an entire community's indebtedness to Saint Joseph. The Brother's presence at the Oratory attracted crowds of people who wanted to show, by their personal offerings, their participation in the collective homage. For pilgrims, donations were both a way of ensuring that the saint would remember them and a manner of practicing detachment, even at the cost of personal hardship. Such self-denial was often the necessary means to reach a life infused with greater meaning, a life more satisfying and more complete. Was it not for this very reason that so many pilgrims came to the Oratory?

Brother André was quite aware of the large sums of money required to complete the construction work and was determined to collect funds. This he sometimes did with startling audacity: after all, he was a humble, a timid, even a reticent man. One has trouble imagining his engaging in any sort of debate with persons of importance, much less persuading them to part with some of their riches.

However, from each of his trips, Brother André would return with a bag full of American currency or checks in Canadian funds. Over time, he raised a considerable amount of money. We cannot put a precise figure on his financial contribution to the cause. Clearly, though, he went to great lengths to assist in the funding of the basilica.

For example, one of his French biographers, Gilbert Phabrey, reports that toward the end of his life, Brother André, by then ninety years old, begged his Superior's permission to go to New York City. He simply argued, "I've never thought of soliciting funds from the great American billionaire John D. Rockefeller. With your permission and blessing, I'll leave tomorrow. . . ." Coming from Brother André, such a request sounds most implausible, yet the tale appears to be authentic.

The next day, the little Brother left for New York City; he never did meet with Rockefeller, who was not in the city at the time. But he was received by Mr. John Burke, the first secretary of the Rockefeller Foundation, who handed him his "biggest check of the year"!

He also entertained a privileged relationship with the Ryan family, great benefactors of the American Church, who were also very generous as regards the Oratory. There were also thousands of anonymous contributors who made discreet, often humble donations whenever they met Brother André. All this goes to show that the Brother recognized how expensive the work on the Oratory would be and never shunned his share of responsibility. He would not rest until Saint Joseph was properly honored in Montreal with the most beautiful, the most breathtaking church on earth.

As fundraising progressed, the commissioned architects, Viau and Venne, finished their drafts. They submitted a preliminary estimate of $2,800,000. The sum was huge, but then so was the proposed building. According to the architectural plans, the structure would be "325 feet long, 192 feet wide, and 467 feet high." It would seat four thousand people; should the chairs be temporarily removed, it would accommodate nine thousand of the faithful. The architectural style was of the Italian Renaissance. The crowning achievement would be the dome, surrounded by a gallery that would serve as an observatory.

The architects' competence was well recognized in Canada. But, considering the exceptional scope of the venture, precautions no less exceptional had to be taken. Mgr. Gauthier, who was very favorable to the project, as we saw earlier on, presented the architectural plans to the committee on architecture of the archdiocese of Montreal. There they were received with unmitigated enthusiasm: "According to the plans submitted to us by the architects, everything seems to have been studied from all possible angles. They have met all the requirements pertinent to the construction of a sanctuary intended not only for popular piety, but also for great displays of faith and for huge pilgrimages."

However, the committee's conclusions were apparently not forceful enough to still the doubts of the diocesan administrator and those of his bishop. Mgr. Bruchési asked that the whole project be submitted to another committee, formed of three French architects of great renown. While the latter praised the plan as a whole, they also suggested several amendments to its design, many of which were eventually implemented.

During the summer, drilling work began. For the future church might well lie on a mountain, it would also be built—literally—on rock, and very hard rock at that. Extremely stable foundations were sunk for this immense basilica, foundations that would carry the weight of a church both wide and high. This proved to be such a challenging enterprise that project engineers sought the advice of a French architect who had worked on the Sacré-Coeur basilica of Montmartre, Paris. One must understand that Quebec had never witnessed construction on such a grand scale: it was only natural to appeal to foreign expertise. For the most part, though, Canadians designed and built the basilica.

On August 31, 1924, everything was ready for the blessing of the cornerstone. That day also marked the third centenary of the consecration of Canada to Saint Joseph. The ceremony was presided over by the Apostolic Delegate, Mgr. Pietro di Maria, who had arrived from Ottawa with good grace: Mgr. di Maria was well known for his personal devotion to Saint Joseph.

On the official platform, ecclesiastical dignitaries, civic officials, and diplomats from several countries gathered in front of a crowd of approximately thirty-five thousand people. Those people were cheering the efforts of the entire Montreal Church. It had been no coincidence that the archbishop himself had paid particular attention to the entire venture. However, in his sermon, the Dominican Father Antonio Lamarche emphasized the role played by the first advocates of this daring architectural endeavor. He spoke directly to the Holy Cross Order:

> Most Reverend Fathers, you shall have the privilege of completing this monument,

just as you had the courage to lay its first stones. You would vigorously refuse this honor—due as it is to your painstaking efforts—if it did not sanction the devotion and glory due to Saint Joseph. You have borne, just as you shall bear again, the slanderous charges of renegades, the reservations of skeptics, and the suspicion of fools or even wise men. You have struggled and shall continue to struggle with financial worries of all kinds. You shall still suffer as you collect alms, even if you collect them only for the Good Lord. You have toiled relentlessly on that laborious task of receiving public or private pilgrimages, and so shall you toil in the years to come. . . ."

Judging from his speech, the good Father must have known Brother André well. And surely the Brother must have noticed the perspicacity of the Dominican's address. His sermon ended with these words: "Your faith in Saint Joseph, dare I say your faith experimental, confirmed by both tangible signs and intimate confidences, shall prevail over future obstacles, just as it has triumphed over difficulties past. . . ."

WORK STOPPAGES

It was no small feat simply to build the substructure of the edifice. To this day, one can still make out, in the basement of the basilica, the different areas where its foundations were laid. To sink the foundations, workers had to dig through layers of solid rock, using huge amounts of explosives. However, the basilica was being built at a stone's throw from one of the wealthiest neighborhoods of the city; dynamite could be used only with the utmost precaution, so as not to rock the adjacent houses.

It was not before May 1926 that the actual construction of the foundations began. A few months later, Father Deguire wrote in the periodical the *Oratory*:

> Over the past weeks, while teams of workers built forms for the concrete, others installed iron rods. Huge pillars and large foundation walls were filled with reinforced concrete. As it now stands, the upper concrete floor is starting to take shape. It will be completed by the end of the fall. The proportions of the entire edifice are staggering and remind us of those immense works of faith, the great cathedrals of Europe. . . .

As winter arrived, work ground to a halt. This necessary respite gave the project administrators some leeway to collect additional funds. It must be noted that, most often, donations came from the source least expected. Witness the discerning remarks of Father Deguire: "Until now, contrary to popular rumor, we have not received any major donations. What has been built so far is due more to the offerings of the poor than to the grants of the rich." No doubt, on occasion, the rich came forth with lavish donations. But it does seem significant that the Oratory was borne of the financial efforts of so many simple folk.

From the very beginning, those people had been the closest to Brother André's heart. He had ministered to them with special attention, and it was with fitting care that they, in turn, laid the financial foundations of the glorious church we see today.

In June 1927, Father Deguire wrote:

> The whole structure will be built in reinforced concrete. This year, the walls and columns will be erected at the height of forty-eight feet along the entire perimeter of the church, except for the apse. Thanks to the generosity of all of the friends of Saint Joseph, $225,000 were collected last year toward construction costs. We never even had to solicit public charity explicitly, nor did we incur the slightest debt. Counting as we do on the renewed beneficence of all citizens, we hope to be able to invest in construction a comparable amount this year.

Despite ongoing construction on the basilica, pilgrims still streamed into the crypt to pray. So much so that in 1928, new and larger parking lots were built to cope with increasing traffic.

Early in 1929, the erection of the supporting walls was completed. The next stage was the installation of the exterior granite walls. A three-year contract of $1,207,254 was concluded with a quarry owner. Over the past five years, construction work had progressed steadily, within schedule and budget. The future seemed bright.

But in October 1929, the New York Stock Market hit a record low. Within days, fear led to panic; the

value of bonds plummeted, wiping out the life sav-
ings of thousands of small investors and bringing
speculators to financial ruin. Entire industries were
bankrupted, factories and shops went out of business, and workers lost their jobs. North America,
the land of opportunity and riches, now struggled
with endemic poverty. Pilgrims came to the Oratory
in ever-larger numbers to beg for the help of Saint
Joseph, the patron saint of the workingman.

On Mount Royal, work went on hesitatingly: after
all, one does not leave an edifice half-built. However,
in May 1931, for the first time since the beginning of
the project, a bank loan had to be negotiated. It totaled
$300,000, with a $100,000 credit margin. This was just
enough money to finish the work already begun, not
to complete the project as a whole. Eventually, workers had to be laid off; they returned to their jobs only
in the summer of 1937.

Despite the work stoppages, those administrators
who had not lost all hope in the project struggled to
find a viable alternative to its original conception. In
January of 1934, Louis-Alphonse Venne died. With
his associate Dalbé Viau, he had been in charge of
the project since its inception. Their architectural
firm had presented its first drafts in 1914. Over the
following twenty years, many changes—essentially
stylistic—had been brought to the initial plans for the
immense sanctuary, but its basic design had never
varied. This is not to say that engineers and architects
had never voiced reservations about certain aspects
of the project, particularly about the proposed dome.
The rigorous Canadian climate was a point in question. Could a dome of such proportions, derived

from European models, withstand the onslaught of Canadian winters? Cost was also an issue. The advice of a French architect of great distinction was sought on the matter.

The architect in question was a Benedictine monk, Dom Paul Bellot. Examples of his work existed in England, Holland, and Belgium, as well as in his own country. The audacity and originality of his architectural style were praised in architectural magazines. He was recognized for his genius in incorporating stylistic elements of the past into modern designs. Also cited was the purity of his line and his experience with construction work in reinforced concrete. He seemed to be the man of the hour.

Not so for Mr. Dalbé Viau, who totally opposed Dom Bellot's architectural style. In this apparently aesthetic dispute, the Oratory authorities sided with the French architect on the questions of both style and cost. As regards style, the French architect's plans for the dome were simpler and more harmonious. As regards money, Dom Bellot's proposal was evaluated at $172,460, while Viau had submitted an initial estimate of $727,974. The figures spoke for themselves, particularly in those days of economic crisis. Viau's contract was cancelled, although the man had devoted twenty years of his life to the construction of the Oratory.

To respect Canadian law governing professional corporations, the French architect chose two Canadian architects as associates: Lucien Parent and Rodolphe Tourville. Despite this agile legal maneuver, Viau launched an appeal against his dismissal, and submitted the case to the Superior General of the

Holy Cross Congregation, Father James Donohue. The latter submitted the dispute to a highly respected American architect, Ralph Cram, who in the past had extolled Dom Bellot's work.

Cram's critical appraisal of the proposed dome was both surprising and acrimonious. Essentially, he argued that, theologically speaking, Bellot's style was unorthodox, and, to borrow his exact wording, "heretical"! Where Bellot saw purity of design, Cram apparently saw revivals of a pagan past and intimations of a godless present:

> Such angles and diagonals seem derived from Aztec or Muslim designs or even Bronze Age works from Mycenæ or Chaldea. . . . I would like to emphasize that this new plan may be fitting for a railway station, for a cinema, for the head-office of a workers' union, or for the temples of one of the new religious denominations that have no historical or doctrinal traditions. But it is not proper for the Catholic Church. . . . I thus instantly recommend to come back to the primitive draft, the rejection of which is presently proposed. It is really a beautiful example of classical work, of architecture excellent in its proportions. It can be recognized instantly as a Catholic church.

The American architect went on to suggest, "May we hope for a *motu proprio* from the Pope establishing the canons of Catholic architecture?"

Thus spoke the American critic, apparently intent on preserving the orthodoxy of American style from the influence of French decadence. One can imagine the effect his harsh words had on his compatriot, the Superior General. The latter simply ordered all work stopped.

Predictably, this decision was greeted unfavorably by the Superior of the Oratory, Father Cousineau, who, in turn, sought counsel from a panel formed exclusively of Canadian architects. They unanimously endorsed Dom Bellot's plans. This was fortunate indeed, inasmuch as the Archbishop of Montreal, Mgr. Gauthier, also thought highly of the Frenchman's proposal. And it was with certain authority that Mgr. Gauthier "advised" Father Cousineau to "stick with Dom Bellot."

The Superior of the Oratory was in an embarrassing position, caught between conflicting allegiances, the one to his Order's Superior General, the other to his archbishop. He suggested a meeting between the two opposing parties. The American Superior half-heartedly rallied to the opinion of the Canadian archbishop and accepted Dom Bellot's plans.

Despite this peaceful arrangement, the wars of architecture quietly simmered within the professional community, and within the Holy Cross Congregation itself, which had closely monitored these disputes of design. The hostilities finally abated when none other than Father Cousineau was elected Superior General of his community.

As all work had been ordered suspended, the basilica stood half-built, roofless, at the mercy of the elements. A few years before his death, Brother André was asked if a roof should be built. He answered, "Put a statue of Saint Joseph in the center of the church, and if he wants a roof over his head, he'll take care of it. . . ."

For some time, the aged Brother had become somewhat detached from the whole business. Brother André was already eighty-seven years old in that fateful year of 1932, when workers had to be laid off because there was no money to guarantee their salaries. Yet he still visited the sick, greeted pilgrims, and traveled occasionally to the United States. And though construction might falter, the faith of the pilgrims never did. All sorts of Catholic organizations, from Montreal, from Canada, from abroad, came on pilgrimages to the Oratory at least once a year. Even in those days, two million people visited the sanctuary every year.

Dom Bellot set to work on what would become one of the biggest domes in the world, after the one crowning St. Peter's of Rome. It was a daunting challenge! Of course, the Benedictine had to design and supervise the construction of a huge dome. But he also had to contrive to erect the dome on walls already standing sixty meters high. At the top of the dome, a lantern and a freestanding eighteen-meter cross would complete the basilica. The surface of the dome had to be weatherproof and specially adapted to the swings of temperature characteristic of the Canadian climate, known for its polar winters and sultry summers. An asphalt joint was located between the base of the dome and its supporting pillars, to allow enough elasticity for the extension of the steel structure. So that the already weighty architectural mass of the basilica would not be too heavy for the tensile strength of the steel supporting it, the dome was built with a concrete mix as thin as it was resistant. The concrete layer of the dome of Saint Joseph's basilica is eighteen times thinner than that of St. Peter's.

To avoid heating and condensation problems, Dom Bellot designed a smaller interior dome that fitted into the larger one, an architectural solution first devised in the fifteenth century for the cathedral of Florence, Santa Maria del Fiore.

Work resumed on the construction site in the summer of 1937. In September 1939, a copper coating was urgently applied to the concrete structure to avoid its deterioration. The Oratory authorities launched one last desperate appeal to their benefactors to ensure that the enterprise would be finished. As it was. On August 31, 1941, the archbishop of Montreal blessed the cross overlooking the whole complex. The exterior of the basilica on Mount Royal had taken on its final shape.

Brother André did not live to see the completed Oratory. The cross was placed over the dome a full four and a half years after his death. He never expressed any regrets regarding "his" unfinished work, for his true labor had always been compassion. To people asking him if the work on the Oratory would be over before his death, he used to reply, "The Good Lord doesn't need me to complete his work. Saint Joseph will see to it."

CHAPTER 11

THOUGHTS AND
COMMENTS

WELL BEFORE HIS death, most people who
met Brother André considered him a saint. Pilgrims
on their return home from the Oratory spread the
word about their personal experience there, or about
the events they had witnessed at the sanctuary. Some
people had met the Brother at the Oratory, others in
the United States or in other Canadian provinces.
Even journalists and reporters fell under his spell—
witness the many articles describing his triumphant
welcome in their cities. Brother André shied away
from the media, though. He detested being photo-
graphed and was loath to be interviewed. Because
of his terrible timidity, he was tongue-tied in front
of strangers, although he might manage to put in a
few words about prayer or devotion. His modesty
virtually forbade him to speak about his own person. To top it off, he was so convinced of playing no
part, personally, in the wondrous events unfolding

around him that he felt he had precious little to say on the subject. If not for the constant reminders: "What nonsense it is, to think that I personally work miracles. . . . It's Saint Joseph who does all the work. . . . I'm only his little dog!"

It would be quite useless, therefore, to sift through newspaper archives in search of some ponderous observation that he might have shared with a journalist. Brother André did not presume to put on paper his reflections, nor did he keep any records of his daily work. So one is left with very little documentary evidence of his faith, of his hopes, or of his perceptions of people and events around him.

Fortunately, some of Brother André's friends had the foresight to record the words he pronounced on chance occasions. They were convinced that one day the Church would recognize him as a saint, and they painstakingly put in writing a few words culled from their meetings or conversations with him. Certain parts of these archives of happenstance are quite arresting and bear careful consideration.

Thus, the Brother commented on the trials he experienced throughout his life: "Nothing of value is easily acquired. When obstacles get in your way, it's a sure sign of success. A difficulty overcome with patience is always followed by a great wealth of graces." Also: "In our prayers, we should not ask to be spared hardship; we should beg for the strength to bear it." His firm belief? "Thank the Good Lord for testing your faith through adversity. If this happens to you, you are lucky indeed. If people could appreciate the true value of suffering, they would call for it on their knees." His reward: "What consoles me is that after each of my trials, the Oratory grew in leaps and bounds." Finally, his hope: "The slightest earthly suffering is rewarded a thousand times over in heaven. If people only realized this, they would fall to their knees and ask to be tried."

Brother André was most tried, in his religious life, when he willingly abided by his Superiors' least enlightened decisions. There were moments when he felt, or thought, that his Superiors did not understand him. Of course, he never even entertained the notion of disobedience. "One should never disobey," he insisted, "even if one is already overburdened with work and still asked to do more." The virtue of obedience was paramount in his religious life; he adhered to its strictest form until the end of his life. Six months before his death, he wondered,

> Maybe I've become too old to be of much good anymore at the Oratory. Maybe I'm in the way. The next time appointments to various positions are made, I'll be happy if my Superiors find me a job where I can still be of some use to the community. Perhaps God expects this last sacrifice from me before my death.

For Brother André, obedience to the rule and to his Superiors was more important than the fate of the Oratory itself.

He welcomed suffering inasmuch as it strengthened his identification with the Lord's Passion. Recall the words he addressed to a young student following the Stations of the Cross with him: "The more you suffer as you follow the Stations of the Cross, the closer you come to Jesus Crucified." This passionate identification with the Galilean was the cornerstone of his spirituality.

This is not to say that Brother André only expressed his love for God through tragic identification. Quite the contrary. He portrayed that love in ways wonderfully human, using refreshingly simple metaphors. He once said to a man,

> What would your wife think if you went a whole month without showing her the slightest sign of affection? She'd think you didn't love her anymore. Your marriage would be in trouble. Well, you see, when you stop going to Communion, the Good Lord also thinks that you have no more love for him. And so now your soul is troubled. . . .

Brother André's devotion to Saint Joseph is well known. But he also often prayed to the Virgin Mary. He said, "When the Virgin Mary and Saint Joseph are both interceding for you, that's a lot of support!" He considered Saint Joseph to be his personal friend, his most trusted confidant; therefore, he used the simple and direct language of friendship when he appealed to him. He even suggested the following prayer to a friend of his who was going though financially trying times: "Good Saint Joseph, please do for me what you would do yourself, were you here on earth, in my shoes, with a large family to support, and business getting you nowhere." His trust in the saint was so great that he stated, "If people prayed with more faith, they'd get all they want from Saint Joseph!"

UNWANTED FAME

Brother André never granted interviews with the calculated enthusiasm of a movie star. But that never stopped journalists from hunting him down and forever detailing his actions and whereabouts. An article published in the *Toronto Star* on November 7, 1930, shows that the little French Canadian's fame had reached Toronto, that bastion of Anglicanism:

> Brother André, the founder of the now celebrated sanctuary of Saint Joseph, is in Toronto. He is a miracle-worker: many wonderful recoveries have been reported by the millions of pilgrims who visit him at the sanctuary. The City of Toronto is presently the host of a man that many consider a saint. We refer of course to Brother André, the founder of Saint Joseph's Oratory, on the slopes of Mount Royal, in Montreal. Last year, more than two million people visited the sanctuary. It has become the Lourdes of this continent.
>
> . . . I met with him, during his two-day visit to Toronto. In a group, he is the man who goes unnoticed. Even at the age of 87, he is a shy, retiring person. No more than five feet tall, he seems even shorter because he always keeps his head bowed. He wears a simple black cassock, bearing no sign whatsoever of ecclesiastical rank. He is now famous, indeed influential, but he has not been given the title of "Father." He remains a humble Brother. He talks neither about his own person nor about the recoveries he brings about.

201

> ... He may well be in this world, but, in
> truth, he is not of this world. He is—of this
> I am convinced—a living saint.

A LIVING SAINT

A journalist attending the Brother's funeral wrote the following lines: "I saw with my own eyes his mortal remains. I watched as thousands of pilgrims paid him their last respects. I felt their passion; I was particularly moved by the piety of a pitifully crippled worker. From then on, I firmly believed in Brother André's sainthood."

Anyone who ever approached the Brother was convinced that he was a saint. Only two weeks after the latter's death, the archbishop of Montreal secretly sent an unofficial letter to the Provincial Superior of the Holy Cross Congregation. In it, he detailed a strategy to hasten the recognition of Brother André's sainthood by Rome. The archbishop wrote:

> Reverend Father,
>
> Will Brother André be canonized one day? We cannot know the Lord's plans for him. However, prudence dictates that we make ready for that possibility. In the normal course of events, beatification procedures can begin only many years after the servant of God's death. In the case of Brother André, if we respect the delays that Rome, in its infinite wisdom, has seen fit to impose, most of the eyewitnesses to his life will have passed on. I thought it wise, in the circumstances, to prepare the

enclosed questionnaire. I suggest you send it to people who knew the Brother well, priests and lay persons alike. For instance, it could be forwarded to his relatives. The recipients should answer the questionnaire in as detailed a fashion as possible and should be encouraged to bring forth every fact and detail, however trivial, that they might remember.

Of course, all people involved in this work should be bound to absolute discretion. It would be most unfortunate if the press got wind of this affair. . . .

This is an ideal way to garner invaluable testimony about Brother André. Should an ecclesiastical court one day sit in Montreal as part of the canonization procedures, witnesses of the time will be able to refresh their memories by drawing on the documentation so compiled.

The writer of this letter, Mgr. Gauthier, died well before his strategy bore fruit. However, some years later, in 1940, Father Cousineau—who was then the Superior General of the Holy Cross Congregation— met with the new Archbishop of Montreal, Mgr. Charbonneau, to consider the possibility of constituting such an ecclesiastical court. After all, Father Deguire, the new Superior of the Oratory, had already appointed a board of inquiry, simply to sift through the countless tales of recoveries that people were bringing to the sanctuary. The board faced the thankless task of attempting to distinguish between factual accounts and stories embellished by religious enthusiasm.

The archbishop was favorable to Father Cousineau's proposal:

> You have brought up the possibility of convoking a trial court in Montreal to pave the way for Brother André's canonization. Such a desire has already been formulated by a good number of priests and believers, and I think it is totally justified. . . . With great joy and total confidence, I hereby accept your request, and presently shall convene such a court.

An ecclesiastical court was instituted, with Father Deguire acting as its postulator. The process got under way in the fall of 1940. Because the Montreal Church had no experience in handling such matters, it took a full three years to hear the testimony of the first thirteen witnesses. But those long-awaited depositions proved to be invaluable.

THE ECCLESIASTICAL COURT

It might be useful to clarify the workings of an ecclesiastical court, especially one adjudicating on matters of canonization. It may seem strange, in such a context, to use the word "court." Indeed, the term is borrowed from the secular judicial system. A secular court, of course, deals with matters of innocence or guilt, not of holiness. It hears the case for the prosecution and that for the defense, and its final authority rests with a judge who must sometimes disregard justice to apply the letter of the law. Obviously, the proceedings of an ecclesiastical court bear only faint resemblance to those of a secular court. This is how the Church adjudicates on matters of holiness: a postulator is deputed to present the plea for the beatification (and eventual canonization) of a candidate; this he does, most often, by calling friendly witnesses. The "devil's advocate" puts the case against beatification, sometimes by pinpointing weaknesses in the postulator's case. The court then weighs the case of both parties. The words "devil's advocate" are now obsolete in judicial terminology, although they have taken on a different acceptance in everyday language. However, the roles of both the postulator and his adversary are well defined, and proceedings leading to beatification are in no way less rigorous than are civil proceedings.

As in any other trial, the choice of witnesses is of great importance. In the case of Brother André, thousands of people could have been called to testify to physical recoveries or spiritual conversions due to his intercession. However, only forty-nine witnesses were summoned. They were selected because of their credibility and because of their intimate knowledge of the life of Brother André, the "servant of God," as a candidate for canonization is called.

Trial courts sat in Montreal; in Ottawa; in Providence, Rhode Island; and in St. Hyacinthe, a small town that lies to the southeast of Montreal, in the very region where Brother André was born. The preliminary mandate of the four courts was simply to gather information. Some of the depositions were quite lengthy. Sister Leblanc, the nun attending Brother André at the end of his life, spoke during eleven three-hour sessions: her deposition is thirty-two pages long. Of course, her testimony is positively concise when we compare it to that of Azarias Claude (forty-five pages), to that of Mgr. Cousineau (seventy-three pages), or to that of Joseph Pichette (eighty-seven pages)! The preliminary trials lasted eight years, from 1941 to 1949.

A great variety of people were involved, people from all ranks of society, people with distinct backgrounds. Of the thirty-two witnesses heard by the court that sat in Montreal, there were eight members of Brother André's religious community, four priests and four Brothers. Also called to testify were the cardinal of Quebec City, the vicar-general of Montreal, and two nuns. All the other witnesses were lay persons. The court heard three doctors, four shopkeepers, a fireman, two businessmen, a pharmacist, a mechanic, two journalists, a contractor, a foreman, a university professor, an accountant, and two housewives.

These witnesses, coming as they did from all walks of life, offered varied insights into Brother André's personality. A laborer would know the Brother in one way; a cardinal or professor would appreciate him entirely differently. Their manifold depositions, when pieced together, enabled the court to grasp a composite portrait of the Brother. Every testimony was accorded equal importance, and the very diversity of the depositions confirmed the credibility of the proceedings.

Unfortunately, for want of space, not all witnesses can be mentioned here, and no single deposition can be quoted in full. These depositions are invaluable, though, inasmuch as they reveal hidden sides of

Brother André's personality. The records of the courts also afford a general appraisal of this man deemed saintly enough to be presented as a candidate for beatification.

Certain excerpts from the depositions are specially revealing. In particular, Joseph Pichette, Brother André's lifetime confidant, spoke of his first meeting with the Brother. At the time, the young shopkeeper suffered from a heart condition so threatening that his physician had advised him to ready himself for "the sweet hereafter." His doctor kindly bade him to seek rest for his body and peace for his soul. Pichette went to Brother André for help; the Brother not only welcomed him, but also shared with him his own room during the length of the treatment. Pichette's testimony allows us to partake in the two men's intimacy; he spoke of the Brother's daily life, of his prayers, of his work, and, presently, of the extraordinary solicitude Brother André showed toward his frail guest:

> There were three of us staying at the chapel at the time. Besides me, there was a young man with a bad leg, who occupied the other bed. As for Brother André, he slept on the floor, on a thin mattress, without even using a pillow. During the first nine days of my stay at the Oratory, there was no change in my condition. Brother André rubbed me with the oil of Saint Joseph two or three times a day. On the ninth day, as I told him there was no improvement, he applied the oil from eleven in the evening to two o'clock in the morning.

This one time, Brother André went down to the chapel. After half an hour, since I had not heard so much as a sound, I went to check on him. He was on his knees, bending his body to the floor with arms crossed over his chest. The next day, Brother André was up at four-thirty in the morning. He had already put some pork and veal to cook on the fire and had peeled some potatoes. He asked me to add them to the stew around ten.

At noon, he came back for lunch. He gave me a huge plate filled with meat, noodles, potatoes, and bouillon. I tried to refuse it, but he insisted, telling me I would feel better if I ate. "Well, since you say so, Brother," I said, "I'll try." He hastily added three thick slices of bread to my fare. After the meal, I felt much better. And Brother André suggested I go for a long walk.

For supper, he served me the same kind of food. I went to bed around ten-thirty, and fell into a deep sleep that lasted until the next morning. This was strange, given that I had not slept a wink since my arrival at the Oratory, nine days earlier, to start my novena. The next day, Brother André said to me, "You're obviously well. No reason for you to stay here any longer."

The heart patient lived to the ripe old age of seventy-eight. In his deposition, he spoke in detail of twenty-six cases of healing he had personally witnessed, as a lifetime companion to Brother André. But he did not dwell on physical recoveries, however spectacular they may have been. He was most impressed by the pilgrims' absolute trust in his old friend: "Of all the people I brought to consult Brother André, none ever left him feeling frustrated. A few were cured, others died shortly after their meeting with him; but Brother André had consoled every last one of them."

Azarias Claude also witnessed several cases of amazing recoveries, which he brought up in court. He mentioned one case in particular, which offers us a glimpse of the Brother's wry—or should we say humble—sense of humor:

> I remember the case of one lady who came to consult Brother André. She could not walk by herself and hung on to the shoulders of the two women who had brought her to the Oratory. Brother André only spoke to her for a very brief moment and then rang the bell to indicate that the meeting was over. The lady rightly felt she had hardly had time to say a word. She rushed past the door, all the while raging against Brother André, who, she claimed, had practically thrown her out of his office. She had failed to notice one thing, in her fury: she had walked out of the office on her own two feet, without the assistance of her companions. Someone brought the fact to her attention. When the women realized what had happened, they all started sobbing. Brother André's petulant caller could now walk with such ease that no one could have guessed she had ever been sick. . . .

When his turn came to testify, Father Cousineau, the Brother's former Superior, chose to speak about

Brother André's religious life, particularly about his humility:

> To my knowledge, Brother André was never vainglorious as regards the phenomenal success of the Oratory. He never even stopped to admire the building, nor did he ever ask one of his guests to acknowledge its beauty. I never heard him say, when he spoke of the Oratory: my labor, my work. Again, to my knowledge, Brother André betrayed not the slightest curiosity concerning the amount of alms or donations collected for its construction. I once attended a religious ceremony at the Oratory. His Excellency Monsignor Gauthier, archbishop of Montreal, said to the guests gathered around him, "If ever I am summoned as a witness for Brother André, I will be able to state, with considerable understatement, that he never put on airs."

Michel Trudel was an accountant, more familiar with the growth of investments than with the flight of the soul. Nonetheless, he was not the kind of man who would blind himself to exceptional manifestations of grace. He testified:

> In my opinion, Brother André practiced the Christian virtues to a degree that was heroic. In the years I knew him, I thought, as I still do, that he lived as a saint. His faith was extraordinary. He liked nothing better than to talk about the Good Lord and the Passion of Jesus. He did so with a fervor that always moved us deeply. His

love of his neighbor was heroic, as regards his attending the sick, despite his failing health and his great age. Even after a hard day's work, he was always ready to visit the sick. He prayed with great faith, especially during the Hour of Adoration of the Blessed Sacrament. His whole life was exemplary. It was Brother André's constant practice of the Christian virtues that struck me the most and made me consider him a saint.

Dr. Lionel Lamy was Brother André's physician. The doctor's whole life had been transformed when he saw his own daughter cured by the Brother. Out of gratitude for this special grace, and out of respect for Brother André's saintliness, he put his whole life at his service. He stated in court:

For ten years, from 1944 to 1954, I headed a medical clinic, with ten specialists acting under me. For years, we analyzed all the medical facts pertaining to the recoveries attributed to Brother André. I referred my own patients to other doctors, in order to devote all my time to this task; I worked on it from nine to twelve and then from two to five every day of the week. . . .

Professor Arthur Saint-Pierre was the director of the Department of Sociology of the University of Montreal. He may well have had the critical eye of the academic, but he could only admire Brother André's detachment from all things material. He spoke kindly about the Brother:

Brother André was totally detached from all material values, such as money and honors. During all of the great ceremonies that I attended at the Oratory, Brother André always stayed in the background.

He was only interested in the expansion of the Oratory inasmuch as it reflected his spiritual concerns. He accepted alms from the pilgrims with unabashed joy simply because he was so happy to be able to hand them over to his Superiors. In fact, he was never so happy as when he brought a large donation to his Superiors. It is as if he had kept the simplicity of a child, despite the extraordinary life he led and the importance of his pastoral activities.

Leone Valente was a foreman, and he knew Brother André very well during the last fifteen years of his life. He left us this depiction of the little Brother:

I was aware that Brother André was in poor health. On several occasions, friends came to my house with the Brother, and they would say to my wife, "Brother André is exhausted; he just can't go on." My wife used to ask him to rest on a makeshift bed in the living room. She would give him a warm blanket and a hot-water bottle for his feet. A half-hour later, my wife would bring him a cup of coffee, which was usually enough to restore his strength. He used to wake from these short slumbers—they might last a half-hour or an hour—-refreshed and invigorated. He even used to claim that he felt as alert as a young man. I never heard Brother André complain about his poor health or even say, "I'm tired." I do not know if his sickliness was a means of purification for him or if it stood in the way of his sanctification. I always knew Brother André with a smile on his face.

Similar depositions go on for hundreds of pages. In their simple, direct, and spontaneous words, Brother André's witnesses spoke of a person they had loved as much for his human qualities as for his spiritual strength.

TESTIMONY
CORROBORATED

The witnesses heard at the trial courts were unanimous in stating that Brother André had practiced the Christian virtues in a heroic way. According to them, he had fully respected his religious commitment by means of his rigorous exercise of obedience and acted with exemplary humility and generosity. However, depositions form only one part of the beatification procedures.

A second step in these procedures began in 1952, when the depositions from the trial courts were sent to the Holy Congregation of Rites, in Rome, along with 245 letters from persons of rank, all promoting the formal institution of the cause at the Vatican. In this respect, Brother André certainly did not lack supporters. The élite of Quebecois society had set to work on his behalf. The Vatican received letters from two cardinals, eight future cardinals, twelve archbishops, and no less than seventy-three bishops! Among the petitioners from the secular realm were the chief justice of the Supreme Court of Canada, the lieutenant-governor of Quebec, and a former Prime Minister of the province. Many well-known personalities from the worlds of politics, culture, and education also appealed to the Vatican in view of furthering Brother André's cause. The formal request was supplemented by a petition signed by 578,861 people!

The letters sent by Canadian bishops bear witness to the popular perception of the humble Brother from Saint-Grégoire. We can only present some brief excerpts from their missives.

> From Mgr. Albini Leblanc, bishop of Gaspé: "This very humble Brother has his place among the great historical figures of the Canadian Church, such as the missionaries and martyrs Brébeuf, Lallemant and Jogues, and the renowned mystic, Marie de l'Incarnation."
>
> From Mgr. Henri Routhier, missionary bishop: "Brother André is, in my opinion, the greatest miracle-worker that the Lord has sent to North America. His renown as a saint, confirmed by the countless blessings owed to his prayer to Saint Joseph, has spread throughout the Americas."
>
> From Mgr. Gérard Coderre, coadjutor of Saint-Jean: "We can no longer keep count of the wonders attributed to Brother André's intercession. In this diocese, the devotion to Saint Joseph, as promoted by

> Brother André at the Oratory, is by far the piety most practiced. In fact, faith in the great saint and trust in the little Brother are linked to such an extent that one can hardly pray to the one without praying to the other."

One should note that even American bishops advocated Brother André's beatification. Cardinal Francis Spellman, archbishop of New York City, wrote to the Vatican: "The faithful of this diocese are convinced that Brother André was a saint. Thousands of them went to see him at Saint Joseph's Oratory, and I am certain they would want me to intercede on his behalf with Your Holiness. . . ."

Mgr. Espelage, of Gallup, New Mexico, sent this letter:

> Brother André's fame spread beyond the borders of his country many years ago. Thousands upon thousands of my compatriots traveled all the way to Montreal to meet with him in person. Sometimes the Brother cured them; often he brought them closer to the Lord. As an American bishop, I cannot be a mere bystander to such events. . . .

By these petitions, bishops showed their solidarity with their flock. Some of them had personally met with Brother André; many more were acquainted only with the testimony of the faithful returning to their diocese after a pilgrimage to the Oratory.

It might seem that, in Quebec, only the prelates of the Church had appealed to the Vatican. As has been stated, the Church was extremely powerful in the province, even in the middle of the century, and its dominion was not confined to the spiritual realm. Most often, only high-ranking governmental officials could voice their opinion on such matters, using their contacts within the Church. There were, of course, some exceptions to this rule. Need one point out, though, that even the most intrepid of laymen would hesitate to convey his concerns directly to the Pope?

From the letters addressed to Rome by laymen, we first quote the words of The Honorable Adélard Godbout, a former Prime Minister of the Province of Quebec—words that came as something of a revelation to observers of the political scene:

> Thirty-six years ago, in 1916, I dislocated my right knee during a sporting event. My leg was set in plaster, but that did nothing to improve my condition. The dislocation was so severe that the slightest movement caused me pain, even in my sleep. I went to see Brother André, who was so confident that I would be cured that he told me to go home directly instead of stopping off at the hospital where I was to be admitted the very next day. I have never suffered from my knee since.

Another letter made its way to the Vatican. It was signed by Etienne Gilson, a member of the French Academy. He is rightly regarded as one of the greatest religious thinkers and historians of this century. As such, we grant his letter the space it deserves:

> Unworthy as I am to bear such witness, and moved only by the search for truth, I request to add my humble testimony to all

those which bear on the venerable Brother André's renown as a saint. . . .

   I speak only as a historical witness, conscious of his responsibilities. I first heard of Brother André's reputed sainthood in Montreal, in 1927. There, many Catholics considered him to be a saint and a thaumaturge. No one voiced the slightest doubt concerning the supernatural gifts he revealed as he guided the souls of those who came to him. The authenticity of his miraculous intercessions—and I greatly regret not having kept a record of them at the time—was commonly held to be beyond dispute.

   From 1929 and 1930 on, I made several long stays in Toronto, a city which Brother André had visited on several occasions. There, I observed—without any particular effort on my part to do so—that the same renown of sainthood was attached to his person, not only among Catholics, but also among Protestants, or to be more precise, in certain Protestant families. To my knowledge, this reputation was never tarnished in any way and lasted until his death.

There were many more letters, many more depositions. The trial was officially instituted in Rome on November 8, 1960. In April 1962, the apostolic trial, the last step in the beatification procedures, was held in the archdiocese of Montreal. On June 12, 1978, His Holiness Pope Paul VI bestowed upon Brother André the title of "Venerable," thus confirming his heroic practice of Christian virtues. After establishing the authenticity of two miracles worked by Brother André, the Vatican decided that the Brother should be beatified.

A magnificent ceremony took place in Rome. On May 23, 1982, in front of thirty thousand pilgrims assembled in St. Peter's Square, Pope John Paul II officially pronounced the Brother blessed. One month later, at the Olympic Stadium of Montreal, fifty thousand people gathered to salute their friend, Brother André. Some had known him personally and remembered a man blessed with immense power, swathed in the utmost simplicity.

What a road he had traveled, from the little village of Saint-Grégoire to St. Peter's Square.

EPILOGUE

IN THE BRIEF chronicles of Canadian history, Brother André represents a unique phenomenon. Indeed, this country has not witnessed the birth of many heroes, of many people of great renown or distinction. Of course, some stars have acquired an international reputation, and by the same token, have spawned a wealth of admirers and fans. They may inspire national pride, or even become role models to some. All countries, all people honor their heroes, and all heroes welcome public acclaim.

With the exception of Brother André. In modern language, he could be called an antihero. He never solicited admiration or honor as such, nor did he ever reap any profit from his unwanted fame. He seemed unable to grasp the very nature of the devotion he inspired in people, and was almost bewildered by the number of people who appealed to him. All his life, he simply did what he thought best: moved by compassion, he unburdened the suffering. Why? Because he loved them. And they requited his love.

There lies the difference between Brother André and other great men. While they may be admired,

Brother André was genuinely loved. And he loved without reserve. There was nothing ethereal about his love; it could almost be called a determined love, a love inseparable from the desire to help, to unburden, and even to heal his neighbor.

And his neighbor was mankind. He welcomed and visited all kinds of people, regardless of their creed, education, extraction, nationality, or social standing. All the people that streamed into his office had one thing in common, though: they were all met with the same considerate affection.

One can only summarize Brother André's work over those long years when he embodied the hopes of millions of people by resorting to the most simple, perhaps the most banal of formulations: he was good to people, he was good for people.

Many pilgrims made public the fact that Brother André had cured them or had been instrumental in their obtaining a special grace. The crutches and canes still on display in both the primitive chapel and the votive chapel of the Oratory afford silent corroboration of these often sensational claims. The witnesses to Brother André's power of intercession are by far outnumbered, though, by those millions of people whose visits were shrouded in discretion. Spectacular events were hardly a matter of routine at the Oratory. Thousands of sick or crippled people went to the Brother for a physical cure and came away with soothed souls. Again, the Brother was good to them; he was good for them.

Recoveries and sometimes even conversions are tangible signs. But how can one measure the spiritual healing that took place at the Oratory? People graced with spiritual blessings were ordinarily very discreet about the matter. They would not, or simply could not, whisper a word about their meeting with Brother André. To the millions of people who visited him at the Oratory, the Brother offered, first and foremost, inner peace; hence the affection people had for him. He gave them a little happiness and hope in a difficult life, especially during the somber years of the Depression. Quite simply, he was good for them.

Up to this day, visitors come to the Oratory primarily in search of inner peace. Several decades after the death of Brother André, millions of people still come every year to the sanctuary to find what he originally dispensed, solace. The intimate bond between the people and Brother André is still at work today, as it was in the past. Throughout the years, it lives on.

PEOPLE FROM HERE AND ABROAD

Today's visitors to the Oratory are quite similar to those of yesteryears. Occasional and regular pilgrims mingle with restless tourists in an atmosphere of singular harmony. Many visitors come from the Montreal area. Some come on a daily or weekly basis, others less frequently. Each year, more than half a million people come to the mountain to celebrate the Eucharist. That figure has not changed since the beginning of the 1980s. With so many of today's churches virtually deserted, how can one explain the perseverance of the faithful at the Oratory? What does it have to offer that ordinary churches do not?

Perhaps pilgrimages, in themselves, bring special meaning to people's lives, meaning that other religious activities do not. Of course, religion no longer plays a large part in most people's daily lives, or in the workings of society. This is a recent, perhaps unique, phenomenon in the history of mankind. For throughout the ages, civilization has gone hand in hand with organized religion. This is not to say that our present-day lives are totally bereft of religious aspirations. Today, people express their spiritual thirst in a manner more individual, in a manner discreet to the point of anonymity. The Oratory remains a sacred place for many people, a place where they can converse with a God that they discover in a personal, rather than in an institutionalized fashion.

People go to the Oratory, as always, to feel God's love for them. However, modern sensibility leans toward personal religious expression: today's pilgrims prefer contemplation to congregation. Private reflection is held to be more rewarding than are formal rites, which are sometimes construed as being artificial or imposed. In this spirit, people approach God as discrete individuals, knowing they will be accepted and loved for what they are, much as they were in Brother André's time.

There is also a wealth of services available at the Oratory that ordinary parish churches simply cannot provide. There are at least seven Eucharistie celebrations per day; and pastoral counseling is available all day long, every day of the year. The setting of the sanctuary still appeals to visitors. Who could fail to appreciate the symbolic ascent of the mountain, the beautiful gardens, and the very expanse of the church, which offers quiet areas for prayer or room for individual contemplation? For harried citizens, the Oratory represents something of a sanctuary, in the secular acceptance of the word.

Places of pilgrimage are indeed essential in urban settings. The theologian André Charron so defines their role:

> They allow for the observance of religious practices which may well be traditional in essence, but are now free of social constraints. They afford a loose structuring of Catholic congregations; they constitute a kind of religious bridge, whereby the individual, without relinquishing the anonymity of the big city, can focus on his personal approach to God. Thus the individual can reclaim certain rites laden with religious meaning, even if these symbolic gestures have disappeared from his daily life.

All of this by no means forbids the attendance of those magnificent ceremonies still held at the Oratory, ceremonies embellished by the harmony of the church's great organ and choir. The week preceding Saint Joseph's feast day is marked by the arrival of thousands of pilgrims, who sometimes travel from faraway parishes and dioceses to attend Mass. Such crowds bring to mind the times of Brother André. In another sense, though, today's visitors to the Oratory do differ from those of times past. People of all creeds and nationalities now come to the Oratory and visibly feel at home there. In some regards, the church has become a nondenominational house of worship, welcoming all those who would approach God. Of course, many people no longer practice any form of religion or express any kind of religious concern. Yet, as it looms over Montreal's skyline, the Oratory still offers a most present sign of divine transcendence in today's secular society.

For believers or agnostics from here or abroad, the Oratory remains a favored site for individual or communal spiritual reflection. As they walk up the mountain, these people leave behind them a some-times stifling and turbulent world. They know such sanctuaries are rare. They know that the Oratory is unique, an exceptional place in a troubled world.

Brother André, for all his power, was not gifted with prophecy. How could he have known the fate of his chapel, how could he have foreseen the changes that have swept over our societies? From the very beginning, though, he wanted Saint Joseph's church to be a place devoted to spiritual edification, to well-being, to sharing and peace. This explains why Brother André's presence can still be felt there, a presence as welcoming and comforting as it was during his life.

TIMELINE

August 9, 1845...............Alfred Bessette is born in Saint-Grégoire d'Iberville, Quebec (then Lower Canada) to Isaac and Clothilde Bessette. He is their eighth child (they will have two more).

1855.................................Isaac Bessette dies while cutting wood in a nearby forest.

1857.................................Clothilde dies of tuberculosis. Alfred is taken in by Clothilde's sister, Marie-Rosalie, and her husband.

1863.................................Alfred moves to the United States, looking for work.

1867.................................Alfred moves back to Canada. He eventually finds his way to Saint-Césaire, where he runs into Father Provençal, a priest-friend from his youth.

November 22, 1870..........Alfred arrives at Notre-Dame College in Montreal with father Provençal's recommendation. He quickly enters the novitiate and becomes a porter. He retains this office most of his life.

1871...................................A provincial council rejects Alfred's candidacy, citing poor health. Alfred is able to convince a loca

August 22, 1872................Alfred takes his first vows.

February 2, 1874...............Alfred Bessette takes his perpetual vows, becoming Brother André. He soon begins interceding for the sick and is the source of many miracles.

1893...................................A new tramway line connects to the College. Brother André uses the tramway stand to receive visitors and listen to the concerns of the sick.

1896...................................The Community purchases a large tract of land, including the facing hillside. André is unable to convince his Superiors to build a chapel there.

1902...................................Brother André falls ill and is bedridden. In the infirmary he convinces the college Superior to allow the building of a chapel dedicated to St. Joseph on the nearby mountain. Brother André begins raising money.

October 19, 1904..............The first chapel is officially opened.

August 1908.....................A new, larger chapel is built to accommodate the growing crowds. It is still not big enough, so a new building is commissioned.

November 22, 1908..........The new chapel is built. The steeple is added in 1910.

1909...................................Brother André is given a private office by the chapel to receive visitors.

January 1914.....................Mgr. Bruchési authorizes the building of a much larger church to replace the already overcrowded chapel.

July 11, 1914.....................The Superior General of the Holy Cross Order grants permission to immediately begin construction of "St. Joseph's Church."

May 11, 1916.....................Boileau Construction Firm is given charge of the construction. Construction begins May 19.

Summer 1917....................Crypt of the church is, by and large, completed. Within a few years, it is deemed too small for the ever-growing crowds.

August 31, 1924................Cornerstone of the church above the crypt is blessed. Construction begins.

1931.....................................Stock market collapses, workers begin to be laid off. Construction halts, although most of the main structure is complete.

January 6, 1937.................Brother André, ninety-one, dies.

1937....................................Construction resumes.

1967....................................The Dome is completed. St. Joseph's Oratory is finally, fully constructed.

May 23, 1982.....................Brother André is pronounced "Blessed" by Pope John Paul II.

INDEX

JEAN-GUY DUBUC is an author, a priest of the diocese of Montreal, and a theologian. He is the former editor-in-chief of *La Presse* in Montreal, and the former president and editor of *La Tribune* of Sherbrooke.

FR. MARIO LACHAPELLE, C.S.C., serves as second assistant general for the Congregation of Holy Cross. He now lives in Rome where he chairs the Inter-Societal Committee on Religious Life and acts as the vice-postulator for the cause of Servant of God André Bessette.

Founded in 1865, Ave Maria Press,
a ministry of the Congregation of
Holy Cross, is a Catholic publishing
company that serves the spiritual and
formative needs of the Church and its
schools, institutions, and ministers;
Christian individuals and families; and
others seeking spiritual nourishment.

For a complete listing of titles from

Ave Maria Press

Sorin Books

Forest of Peace

Christian Classics

visit www.avemariapress.com

ave maria press / Notre Dame, IN 46556
A Ministry of the Indiana Province of Holy Cross